My Child Is Angry... And So Am I

Phil —
your friendship and peer
advisement has been invaluable
Thank you for all that we shared
may you find the book
intriguing and useful for
helping others. Enjoy the read
and keep expanding
your vision
Dave

My Child Is Angry...
And So Am I

Guiding Youth in Expressing Anger Constructively

Dr. David R. Leaman

ISBN: 1515018075
ISBN 13: 9781515018070
Library of Congress Control Number: 2015911445
CreateSpace Independent Publishing Platform
North Charleston, South Carolina

To my loving wife, Joyce. In our forty-five years of marriage, she has been my love, my teammate, my cheerleader, and my colleague. Without her *countless hours* of support—especially typing, editing, and critiquing—this book would not be possible.

Contents

Anger Is Necessary

We were driving to our destination in obscurity. My wife had a vague idea of where we were going. I did not have a clue. We were beginning to feel anxious because we were running late, and we needed to be there soon. My wife would not reveal our final destination, because it was supposed to be a big surprise. She had told me that for my birthday, she was going to take me to a place I had never been, to see friends from the past whom I had not seen for a long time. All I had to do was drive the car, and she would navigate.

Unfortunately, our "surprise friend" forgot to give my wife the directions, so when we left the house that morning, my wife was blindly hoping she could guide us to the right place. Three hours later we were lost on a country road in Lancaster County, Pennsylvania. The beauty of the Amish countryside could not diminish my growing frustrations. We were lost, but the "GPS" beside me kept her lips locked—all for the sake of surprise. She finally conceded to let me ask someone for directions, so I pulled up to a four-way stop sign surrounded by farmland. I flagged down a man in a pickup truck and asked, "Do you know where Salunga is?"

He paused, gave me a very strange look, and replied, "Buddy, you're *in* Salunga!"

"Oh, really," I choked out. There was nothing within my vision except two houses and some cornfields.

He inquired, "What're you lookin' for?"

I replied quizzically, "I don't know."

The man looked at me as though he was talking to an idiot. Maybe he was. He tried again, asking, "Where is your destination?"

I hesitated and then meekly stated, "I don't know. My wife didn't tell me."

The man shook his head and said with exasperation, "Buddy, you need a lot more help than what I can give you!" And with that, he spun his tires and abruptly drove off.

His words still continue to echo in my mind: "You need a lot more help than what I can give you!" How often, as parents and caring adults, we can identify with the reality of needing more help. This is particularly true when we try to assist our children in managing angry, hostile feelings. Too often in the expression of anger, adults get locked into power struggles with children, and the conflict escalates into ugly, painful scenarios. Many adults simply do not know how to express anger constructively. Their lack of knowledge and practical skills results in actions that make interactions worse. Not only are they ineffective in helping their angry child, but also their attempts to intervene frustrate the child even further.

Consider the interaction between parent and child in the following episode:

Dan came home from school, slammed his books on the kitchen table, threw his sweatshirt on the floor, and stomped up to his bedroom.

The parent shouted, "Get back down here, and put your stuff where it belongs—not in the kitchen!"

Dan came downstairs, mumbling, grabbed his sweatshirt and climbed the steps again.

The parent confronted him more loudly. "Pick up your books too! What is your problem, anyway?"

Dan shouted, "Nothing! Just leave me alone."

The parent challenged him. "Don't talk to me that way. I asked you a question, and I demand an answer."

Dan snapped back, "It's none of your business. I hate school; I can't stand the stupid English teacher. She is such a jerk!"

The parent retorted and said, "You have a lousy attitude, and you are disrespectful! Somehow you always screw things up."

The teen yelled, ""I've had enough! Just get out of my life." He walked outside, slamming the door with a loud bang, and disappeared.

The parent gaped in bewilderment.

In this example, both the parent and the teen exhibit destructive actions. Their anger and mutual sense of helplessness erode the relationship. Neither knew how to reduce the emotional tension or use effective problem-solving strategies. What could they do differently to prevent angry escalation and find a practical solution?

The focus of this book is twofold. One purpose is to help parents and other adults learn about themselves and alter how they personally handle their own anger. The mistakes that people make in relating to children are usually an extension of their own unresolved conflicts. Adults can learn to comprehend the meaning and function of their own anger and then modify their actions appropriately. The content and exercises discussed in this book are designed to achieve that purpose.

The second focus is to assist adults in teaching effective anger management skills to children. The concepts and skills are practical. A systematic approach utilizing cognitive behavioral strategies is carefully delineated. The reader will be given a rationale for each strategy and clear guidelines for how to use the skill in helping children. The book is practical but not a simple cookbook of directions.

I recall an incident when my three-and-a-half-year-old granddaughter wanted to help her mother make breakfast. They decided to make pancakes. The child was pretending to read the directions on the pancake box. Her mother asked, "What do the directions say?"

Without hesitation, the child gleefully answered, "The *'rerections'* say, 'Bake the pancakes, den eat 'em.'" If only our complex emotional problems could be solved by simple box directions like that!

In chapter 12 of this book, a more clinical section is provided for mental health professionals and educators. This part will include a detailed description for conducting anger management groups. Therapeutic procedures and techniques will be described explicitly, with practical suggestions on how to teach each skill in a group setting.

Defining Anger

When you hear the word "anger," what comes to your mind first? What do you picture?

When I ask that question at anger anger management seminars, some common responses are "yelling," "explosion," "out of control," "conflicts," and "hurts." Almost always anger is viewed as a negative, destructive force. Most of us have been on the receiving end of angry outbursts and recall the emotional pain coming out of that kind of venting. We seldom think about anger in a constructive manner—as a vehicle for solving problems.

What is anger? What is a practical definition of anger? It has been defined in a variety of ways. Howard Kassinove and Raymond Tafrate, leading psychological researchers, define anger as:

> A privately held emotional state of varying intensity, with associated verbal and motor behaviors, bodily responses, cognitive distortions and deficits, verbal labels, and interpersonal effects.[1]

Another psychologist who has made significant contributions in developing anger management strategies is Ronald Potter- Efron. In a recent book, he simply defined anger as "an emotional state that can range in intensity from mild irritation to extreme rage."[2] The *Webster* dictionary defines anger as "a feeling of great displeasure or hostility."

When considering these varied definitions, two common elements can be identified:

1. Anger is an uncomfortable emotion with a range of intensities.
2. Anger is aroused when individuals detect a potentially distressing or conflicting situation.

Researchers describe anger in terms of biochemical responses to a perceived threatening stimulus. Many anger management programs are based on anger arousal models that use cognitive behavioral strategies. One of the most comprehensive anger-control programs has been developed by

Jim Larson and John Lockman.[3] They have developed an empirically based program for schools, training teachers to use emotional-regulation skills in the classrooms. They note that aggressive behaviors are in part due to an inability to regulate emotional responses to anger-provoking situations.

My concise summary definition of anger is "a biochemical response to a perceived threat." When our brain computes that a present situation could be threatening, we experience an immediate biochemical reaction. The limbic system of the brain fires a message to the adrenal gland, preparing for action. More specifically, the thalamus in our midbrain signals the amygdala, which directly triggers the autonomic adrenal response. There is a limbic surge of adrenaline and catecholamines that produce a fight-or-flight response. The cardiovascular surge immediately produces chemical and muscular changes in the body. Heart rate is increased, blood pressure is elevated, and respiration changes to quicker and shorter breaths. Dizziness, sweating, nausea, and muscle tension in the arms and legs are common ways anger is manifested in the body. These physiological changes occur automatically. The intensity of these abrupt changes is proportional to the amount of adrenaline and other chemicals charging through our bodies. It is an emotional reaction that does not involve conscious thinking initially but results in a physical surge of energy. When anger occurs we can feel the sensations in our bodies.For example, imagine that while walking down a street by yourself, you notice two men following you. Upon closer observation you see that one of them has a knife and the other has a big, mean German shepherd dog. They are looking at you menacingly. At that moment of realization, your brain computes potential danger, and the limbic system triggers the adrenal fight-or-flight response. Your body is immediately prepared to either fight for your life or run like crazy.

At the time of anger arousal, the thalamus also signals the neocortex of the brain, which processes the stimulus quickly. It selects a possible response to the perceived threat based on past learning.

In addition to our biochemical reactions, angry actions can also be described as socially learned over time. We learn what to be angry about and how to express that anger. The stimuli that trigger the limbic surge or fight-or-flight response vary between cultures and individuals. So what one person becomes angry about may not trigger an angry response in someone else. The triggers of anger arousal are unique to the person and cultural expectations. How an individual expresses anger can be modified through personal experience.

It is easy to understand anger in dangerous situations. But it is not so apparent in social situations where there is no threat of physical harm. Suppose you are verbalizing a strong personal opinion, and someone disagrees with you. The person maliciously comments, "Why don't you just shut up? You don't have anything worthwhile to say.?" Immediately you will experience a biochemical fight-or-flight reaction in your body. To some degree you feel threatened emotionally. Your sense of worth is questioned, and the perceived threat will trigger an angry response. Although not in physical danger, you feel angry and ready to fight. But you have a variety of behavioral options. You don't *have* to punch the person although you *feel* like doing so. Neither do you have to attack verbally. But you do have to take *some* action in order to channel the aggressive urges.

From this discussion it should be apparent that having the emotion of anger is not wrong. Angry feelings are a vital part of our existence, designed to help us survive and also cope with distress. We can experience very intense anger and still make healthy choices in expressing it. How we show anger can be evaluated as either good or bad. What we do with our anger constitutes moral behavior, not the feeling of angry emotion. Consider the words of the apostle Paul, quoting from the psalmist who wrote, "Be angry and sin not."[4] The challenge is not to eliminate anger but rather to learn how to channel that emotion and energy into constructive action.

CHAPTER 1

Personal Reflection Activities

1. Think about your life experiences during the last two months.

    *   Identify two occasions in which you felt angry.

    *   Write down the events of the angry episode.

2. Identify what types of events usually provoke anger in you most easily.

    *   Are you more likely to get angry at things or people?

3. Consider your children.

    *   Identify what typically angers each child.

    *   Are there similarities between you and each child regarding what evokes anger?

4. In your family of origin, how did your parents define anger?

    *   Were you allowed to express anger, or was anger viewed as wrong?

CHAPTER 1

Exercises to Help Children

1. What does your child picture or visualize with the word "anger"?

    - Encourage each child to draw a picture of a time when he or she experienced anger or witnessed someone showing anger.

    - Ask each child to identify words or images that come to mind about anger.

2. What colors does your child associate with anger? You may want to encourage your child to express anger in painting or drawing.

3. Invite all family members to suggest some definitions of anger by asking each to complete the following sentences:

    a. "Anger is…"

    b. "Anger is like…"

    - Afterward, record their contributions into a composite family definition of anger and post it in a visible place.

- Compare your family definition with the concept of "Anger is a biochemical reaction to a perceived threat."

4. Ask each child to complete the following sentence with at least three different responses: "I get angry about..."

5. Prepare eight to ten strips of paper with a different emotion written on each. Make sure that anger is one of the emotions included. Invite family members to play a charade-style game in the following way:

    - Each person draws a paper strip and then acts out the emotion using props while the others try to guess the emotion.

    - After each family member's turn, the parent simply asks, "Is it wrong to express or show that emotion?"

    - At the end of the game, discuss with your children that anger is also an acceptable emotion and is not bad.

    - Consider the scripture in Ephesians 4:26 for the discussion.

CHAPTER 2

Roots of Anger

MOST INDIVIDUALS READING this book have not been physically threatened during the last several months. Your life has not recently been endangered by something or someone trying to harm you. However, you probably have been angry and maybe even explosive.

If we are not actually facing a real threat to our bodies, why do we still become angry? Why do we get angry when our child refuses to follow our commands or rules? When a friend or partner deceives and betrays us, we feel angry. What is that about?

The definition of anger used in this book is "a biochemical reaction to a perceived threat." It could be a social threat that challenges our sense of worth or value. Most of our anger is triggered in social interactions, when there is not an obvious physical threat. We experience emotional pain that is then manifested in angry actions. We could assume that deeper roots of anger exist.

Perhaps a way to conceptualize the roots of anger is to think of a tree. Above ground one sees the trunk, branches, and leaves. The growth of the tree is obvious, but beneath the surface are the unseen roots. Roots underground are vital to sustaining the life of the tree. Without the roots there could be no growth. So it is with anger. Regarding the overt behavior, one sees the outward expressions of anger but may not be able to identify its source or roots. People may experience angry feelings but do not have a clue about the cause. The roots are the deeper emotions, which are painful and difficult to identify. The roots provide the vitality of anger.

If one desires to change angry actions, the deeper roots need to be identified and understood. The deeper roots are associated with human vulnerabilities. It is easier to suppress or deny negative feelings than to own and express them. Emotional pain is distressing. We naturally do not want to feel emotional discomfort. Thus, we tend to express anger outwardly rather than to feel the deeper emotional root. We are likely to manifest anger instead of expressing the emotional pain beneath the anger.

Psychological research supports the concept of anger roots. In 1993, Sandra Thomas published a significant book investigating anger and women. The author identified several underlying social causes of anger and aggression. Her research included a comprehensive interview of over five hundred women. In the survey Thomas found that women identified three primary sources of anger. One root was hurt or injustices done to them. They also identified feelings of powerlessness as a source of anger as well as irresponsible actions of others.[1] Thus, deeper emotions of hurt and helplessness were recognized as the roots of anger.

Steven Stosny, another contemporary psychologist, concludes that anger is a reaction to physical or psychological pain. A primary purpose of anger is to numb the painful feelings of hurt. He identifies core hurts that emerge from being disregarded, devalued, and rejected. Stosny further suggests that anger alienates the individual from knowing one's true inner experience. Angry reactions are an attempt to stop pain and control the environment. However, actions that spring from anger and resentment do not succeed in curing the deeper wounds and eventually increase our sense of failure.[2]

Based upon psychological research and my anecdotal clinical experience, I propose that four deeper emotions form the roots of anger. During my years as a psychologist, I have discussed four roots of anger with clients. They include the following: hurt, powerlessness or inadequacy, anxiety about losing something important, and guilt. When one or more of these painful emotions are triggered, the individual is likely to manifest angry behavior. Rather than feel the pain, anger is expressed. People will show aggression and blame others in place of feeling and dealing with the uncomfortable psychological pain.

I believe that understanding these concepts can enable a person to get in touch with inner discomfort. With honest self-analysis we can identify the deeper roots of anger, own our feelings, and modify our actions.

Hurt

Perhaps the most common root of anger is hurt. What one experiences as hurt is unique, so other people may not feel hurt by the same stimulus. There are a variety of ways that we can be emotionally hurt. For example, when someone calls us a derogatory name or puts us down, we are likely to suppress the pain and show hostility. People may observe our angry response but not know the hurt we feel deep inside. The root of our anger is the emotional wound.

Consider the following situation. You and your partner go to a social event or party together. Your partner becomes enamored by a younger, attractive person of the opposite sex. Your partner seems flattered by the attention from the other person. You are ignored as your partner spends considerable time talking and laughing with the other person. If you care about your relationship, most likely you will feel hurt. How would you express or show your emotions? Many people would express the hurt in some angry manner. Perhaps in the car on the way home, you might verbally attack your partner with such phrases as, "You're a jerk! You ignored me all night while you flirted with someone else. If you ever treat me like that again, I'll leave you, and I won't look back. You made a fool of yourself in public. I want nothing to do with you. Just get out of my life."

We can fling out fighting words. We show our anger but conceal the deeper emotion of hurt in such a moment. Our anger feels like a temporary protection and release for the tension in our bodies. Unfortunately such angry expressions do not foster meaningful dialogue nor lead to effective problem solving. Often those cutting words lead to the escalation of hostilities, resulting in more scars and deeper wounds.

Many adolescents respond with angry outbursts when they feel put down. Name-calling or teasing can be the trigger that leads to a physical fight. Feeling misunderstood for having an opinion disregarded can trigger a fight-or-flight response. Typically teens react with anger instead of showing the hurt. Different social experiences can produce hurt feelings. People can feel hurt by being neglected or deserted. Broken promises are hurtful. Perhaps the most excruciating hurts are betrayals and rejections. When we experience wounds caused by people who are supposed to love us, the pain can be excruciating. Anger may be expressed in the form of rage, but the deeper emotion is profound hurt.

Here is another example to consider. A twelve-year-old boy verbalized anger about his father. His parents reported that during the last several months he had cursed his father, broken furniture, and punched a younger sibling. He was very vocal about disliking his father and stated that he would never trust his dad again. Upon further exploration the boy related that his father promised to take him fishing the first day of trout season. However, when the day arrived, his father made plans to help a neighbor replace the roof of his house. The father explained that he could go fishing the following Saturday. But that day came and they did not go fishing because the dad was busy with another project. It was now July. Many Saturdays had come and gone, and the boy had not yet gone fishing. He spit out the words, "I hate my dad. I will never believe what he says." The father's broken promises had deeply wounded the boy. Although the hurt was very real, the boy didn't reveal his pain, but he certainly displayed anger. It is easier to show anger than hurt. If the hurt is not recognized and appropriately handled, anger will continue and probably escalate over time.

Helplessness

A second deeper emotion usually manifested as anger is helplessness. When a person does not know what to do or how to fix a problem, feelings of inadequacy emerge. The adrenaline response can be fired while trying to put something together. Think of the frustration of reading unclear directions when assembling some kit or project. Often we experience minor situations in which we cannot immediately solve the problem, such as unexpected traffic delays, computer glitches, machines that don't operate correctly, incompetent service representatives, and disobedient children. How angry do we become in such moments? Our typical response is to yell or curse or become aggressive. Some of our most painful social experiences occur when somebody is aggravating us, and we can't control the situation.

Young and inexperienced parents can feel overwhelming helplessness at the incessant crying of a colicky baby. No matter what efforts they exert in trying to comfort the infant, the baby continues to wail. In utter helplessness the parent screams at the child and shakes her. That moment of aggression produces irreversible damages for the baby and caretaker. The parent is labeled as a child abuser and faces dire consequences. The infant experiences critical brain injuries. The surface emotion was rage, but the deeper feeling was intense helplessness.

While working therapeutically with married couples, I have observed angry outbursts. Frequently the anger erupts when a person feels helpless to change the undesirable behavior of another person. Men, particularly, express rage when they feel trapped. A caring wife may attempt to coerce her husband into talking. She may be too critical in her efforts to improve him. The husband, who has difficulty expressing his thoughts clearly, feels overwhelmed when pressured to talk. In that moment his adrenaline is rapidly escalating. As the pressure mounts, he feels helpless and finally explodes in rage. The explosion frightens his wife, who abruptly retreats. The problem remains unresolved, with both people more dissatisfied. Many men feel inadequate when it comes to communicating and expressing emotions. The sense of helplessness can lead to explosive outbursts.

Another example is a teenager sitting in the classroom, wishing she were anywhere but there, when she's handed a worksheet to be completed in class. The girl looks at the directions but does not understand. She has no clue about how to complete the assignment. So she shoves the paper away and mumbles about the stupid assignment and refuses to try. The teacher sternly confronts her and orders her to do the work. She reacts with an angry outburst. The teacher then sends the teen to the office for inappropriate and disruptive behavior. However, the real core to those angry actions is her deep feeling of inadequacy. It's too embarrassing and painful for her to admit ignorance. Helpless feelings unravel into aggression.

Owning our sense of helplessness in certain circumstances is difficult. It is painful to admit that we cannot do a task or don't understand a concept. It is much easier to show anger than ask for help. Frequently we express anger from feelings of helplessness and blame someone else. Yelling and blaming gives us temporary relief, but it solves nothing.

Anxiety about Losing Something of Value

A third, deeper root to anger is more subtle and harder to recognize than either hurt or helplessness. It is not fear of physical harm but the anxiety related to our perception that we might lose something. The possibility of losing status, recognition, or an important relationship causes anxious feelings. We are likely to show anger when an important possession is at risk of getting damaged.

For example, suppose you are given a project at work to develop and complete. With the assignment comes a lot of responsibility, but it holds the expectations of recognition for achievements and a probable pay increase. You work hard for several months developing the product. One coworker assists you periodically, but you are the brains and prime mover in the project. When the project is completed, your supervisors are pleased. In fact, they take your ideas and implement them immediately. Unfortunately they give recognition and credit to the other person. The coworker who made a minor contribution gets the credit. You do not receive the recognition for your creativity and dedicated work. You do not receive a financial reward for your efforts. Instead your coworker gets those rewards.

How do you feel? Your body will experience a surge of adrenaline. Although you are in no physical danger, the social and emotional pain is real. You've lost something valuable. What was rightfully yours was taken.

The anticipation of losing something important can be a powerful root of anger. When something that you value is threatened, such as an important possession or your reputation, anger emerges.

In middle school, preteens face the immense challenge of being accepted. Trying to find a group in which to belong is crucial for social adjustments. The bickering and backbiting among peers can be vicious. Younger teens who are driven by survival anxiety try to be cool and fit into an ever-changing and confusing world. A common fear of teens is about losing status with their identified subgroup. Any action exhibited by an adult or peer that might potentially threaten their acceptance can ignite an explosion. Parents and teachers may be confused about why preteens react with aggression over minor incidents. The child's fear of embarrassment packs a powerful punch. A teen is not likely to share the underlying anxiety but will display overt anger. The preteen child may not have the ability to identify what really triggers the anger, but the core issue is fear of losing social status.

Guilt

The fourth root of anger is guilt, which is experienced when someone gets caught doing wrong. It is uncomfortable when our wrongdoing is exposed. We often react with anger, and our natural response is to blame others or verbally attack them. Perhaps the prototype example of that is found in the biblical text about Adam and Eve.

When God questions Adam about the fruit, Adam blames his wife. When God confronts Eve, she blames the serpent. All mankind continues the pattern of blaming others when personal guilt is exposed. Often angry behavior accompanies the feelings of guilt. We can quickly act with hostility toward the one who exposed our wrongdoing.

Fred is a typical sixteen-year-old boy. He asked his parents if he could drive their car to a friend's house. His mother reluctantly permitted this but insisted that he only drive to his friend's house and that he be home by 11:00 p.m. The boy agreed and drove off. A couple of hours later, his mother's intuition kicked in. She had an uneasy feeling about Fred speaking the truth. She called the friend's house and talked to a parent to inquire about him. She was informed that they had not seen Fred. Eventually Fred arrived home at 11:30 p.m. His mother met him at the door and asked where he had been. Fred insisted that he was at his friend's house and even challenged her to call the friend. His mother revealed the truth, and Fred was busted for lying and breaking their agreement. Fred threw down the keys and exploded. "You treat me like a baby! Your rules suck! You don't trust me, and you're always checking up on me!" He stomped off, cursing under his breath. The anger is obvious, but the emotional pain of guilt is not.

It is much easier to show anger than to feel guilt. It is easier to attack and blame than to admit and apologize when there is a perceived threat initiated by exposed guilt.

Another example is a married woman who was secretly communicating through the Internet with a man whom she had not yet met in person. Their texting and e-mailing progressed to include erotic messages. They planned to rendezvous in the near future. Her oldest son was savvy enough to discover what was happening, and he talked with his father. They printed out some of the messages, and the husband privately confronted her. When shown the evidence of the sexual messages she had exchanged with the man, his wife responded with anger, accusing him of invading her privacy. She hurled ugly words and yelled that he was controlling and impossible to live with. She angrily pointed out that he was no saint and, with stinging comments, threatened to leave. The anger is obvious. The guilt has been exposed.

In summary, anger has deeper social roots. Like a tree, angry actions are above the surface. Deeper emotional roots that feed the anger are below the surface. At least four deeper roots can be identified: hurt, helplessness, anxiety of losing something important, and guilt. When you feel anger arise, ask yourself about the root of your anger. Can you identify the deeper root in that particular situation? It is helpful to name the underlying source of anger. Would you be willing to verbalize the deeper emotion instead of manifesting angry actions?

CHAPTER 2

Personal Reflection Activities

1. Refer to the previous chapter where you wrote down a personal angry situation.

   • Think about the incident.

   • Can you identify what the deeper emotional root was?

   • Which of the four roots were fueling your anger? (Sometimes it can involve two or more roots.)

2. Which anger root is most often beneath your aggressive actions?

3. Which parent or sibling hurt you the most as a child? How did you respond?

4. During the next month, try to identify what your deeper root of anger is in each incident of anger.

   • Additionally, when a family member shows overt hostility, try to assess what deeper root the person might be experiencing.

   • What could happen if you focused on responding to the other person's deeper emotional pain instead of reacting to the overt angry actions?

CHAPTER 2

Exercises to Help Children

1. Draw a tree with four roots, or have your child draw it.

    • Name the drawing the "Anger Tree."

    • Discuss the concept that the angry behavior you witness in your child is like a tree above the ground.

    • Draw the analogy that beneath the surface around a tree are roots that feed the tree. The Anger Tree is fed by emotional roots.

    • Give examples of emotional roots that feed some people's anger.

2. Ask your child to try to identify the deeper root in the angry situations written down in the previous chapter.

    • Discuss different ways that people can feel hurt, including put-downs, broken promises, rejection, and betrayals.

    • Explain to your child that most people show angry behavior when they feel hurt, and it is hard to recognize our hurts immediately.

3. During the next two weeks, prompt your child to write down each angry situation. Keep a chart listing the child's angry experience. Discuss each situation with the child and identify the deeper root in each event.

4. Ask the child how he or she may have felt hurt in your family. Let the child know that it is safe to be honest so that relationships can improve at home. Can you let the child know that you will genuinely try to recognize his or her hurts and seek to reduce them?

CHAPTER 3

Recognize and Accept Your Anger

ANGER CAN BE likened to a river. The flowing water is contained and guided by two banks. As long as the river stays within the banks, water provides many useful functions. One can play in the water, swim, or float with the current. A variety of water sports can be enjoyed on the river. The flowing water is relaxing and soothing to the soul. However, if the river floods and rises above the banks, disastrous things can happen. The peaceful river becomes a raging torrent that can destroy and demolish. It is then a liability, not an asset.

Likewise, anger contained appropriately within the "banks" of guiding principles can be very useful. Positive angry energy directed effectively can accomplish significant solutions or strengthen relationships. But anger that floods uncontrollably can cause immense damage and destroy relationships. Unchecked anger is hazardous to your health and a risk to society.

What are the two guiding banks necessary to channel anger appropriately? These banks are skills that enable people to constructively use anger to solve problems and enhance relationships. When these banks are not put in place, anger flooding occurs.

Positive thoughts or healthy cognitions form one bank in the river of anger. Certain specific cognitions have the power to channel anger effectively toward meaningful goals. What a person thinks and repeats in the mind influences the actions expressed. Our self-talk impacts the intensity of emotions and influences our choices. Negative or irrational thoughts escalate anger, but healthy, appropriate self-talk calms and modulates it.

The other bank consists of constructive actions used to inhibit escalation and provide effective problem-solving tactics. These actions include changes in breathing and behaviors to reduce tension in the muscles. People can unlearn former ineffective actions and develop healthy cognitions and behaviors. New neural pathways can be established in the brain with significant positive changes. Essentially, anger management consists of teaching constructive thought patterns and behaviors that prevent anger escalation and use creative problem-solving skills.

Imagine a ten-point scale and label it "my anger scale." Everyone moves up and down the scale daily according to the degree of anger experienced. At the lower end, a small amount of adrenaline is triggered when a person becomes angry. You may notice a slight irritation in a mildly bothersome situation. Your physiological response is minimal, with a subtle change of breathing, a slight increase in heart rate, and a little more muscle tension. An example for some might be an interrupting phone call from a telemarketer or a fly that keeps buzzing around. In the middle ranges, the intensity of your anger is greater, and the distressing situation is more significant. You can definitely feel muscle tension and are more likely to raise your voice and manifest some aggressive action. You feel physical sensations and a greater urgency to do something to reduce your discomfort. You are more prone to use critical words and a judgmental tone. At the nine or ten point, the out-of-control range is reached when your anger is so high that you yell, hit, or throw things. You use hostile or threatening comments and behave unreasonably. There is no rational problem solving, only aggression coursing through your body. You look and act out of control. Biochemically, the frontal lobes of the brain and neocortex are subdued. Your primitive, instinctive brain stem is dominating in that moment. Sheer aggression has taken over like a reflex action. You can't control it. It is a biochemical reaction built into your brain for survival. Steven Stosny's metaphorical description of this moment is "trying to put out a light by throwing a rock at it."[1] It does succeed in putting out the light, but it causes destruction in the process. When the adrenaline reaches a certain accumulated point in your body, the reasoning, creative, problem-solving neocortex shuts down while the primitive brain takes over with powerful aggressive force. Someone once humorously described these moments as follows: "I'm brain-dead; my left brain is not right, and my right brain has nothing left."

The initial goal of anger management is to prevent escalation toward a nine or ten on the anger scale. Relationships suffer and damage repair is needed if we allow such escalation. Sometimes it takes days or weeks to heal the emotional damage inflicted in one moment of a ten-point level of anger.

In my seminars I discuss a "crazy eight" point as the imaginary level of intensity that fires unreasonable aggression. The amount of accumulated adrenaline and other chemicals released into the body can reach a critical point. At that time, the ability to reason and problem solve is significantly compromised. The tension in the body and degree of angry sensation is so high that the aggression switch fires and hostile actions explode indiscriminately so that whatever or whoever is nearby gets attacked. Every one of us is capable of reaching the crazy eight point if we allow the accumulated chemicals to escalate too high. People who allow anger to escalate quickly develop a pattern of aggressive reactions. However, we can all learn to monitor ourselves and reduce explosive outbursts. It can be helpful to label your anger and rate each incident on the anger scale. Children and teens also can learn to rate the intensity of anger and assign a number ranging from one to ten. This rating makes us more aware of our anger and the potential for negative escalation.

Another important step in managing anger is to recognize where in your body you experience the initial tension. Manufacturers of cereal boxes once enticed children by asking the question, "Where's Waldo?" Children were fascinated and entertained looking for that little graphic of Waldo. In a similar way, one might ask, "Where is the tension in my body?" When adrenaline is released into our bodies, there are observable physiological changes and certain muscle groups increase tension immediately. This tension can be generalized through the body, but it also becomes localized in specific muscles.

Ask yourself this question: "Where in my body do I first notice tension when I get angry? What part of my body signals tension when the adrenaline surge is released?" There are different locations among individuals. For example some people first notice tension in the extremities, with a clenched fist. Another person might first notice tightness in the chest or racing heart palpitations. For someone else it might be nausea in the stomach or tight muscles in the forehead.

Most people are oblivious to their body sensations. Some will say they get tense all over. There is truth to that statement, but usually with careful observation one can identify a specific muscle group that manifests the most tension. That self-awareness can provide immediate personal information about anger. By becoming aware of body sensations related to adrenaline, you can recognize the escalation of your anger.

Recognizing adrenaline-induced body sensations calls for a quick, appropriate response. It is like a traffic signal that flashes yellow. What is the purpose of the yellow traffic light? It provides a caution and warns us to slow down. Prepare to decelerate and stop! Of course, for some of us, the adolescent urge is to step on the gas and speed through. A person can ignore this yellow caution, but there may be consequences to pay.

When I was younger, I did not pay attention to my body. As an adult, while taking a graduate course on relaxation response, I started to notice my body sensations. I began to observe my breathing and muscle tension in various situations. One day, while driving a car around the beltway of a big metropolis, I got a headache in my forehead and facial muscles. My training in body awareness paid off. I dutifully observed and noticed that my jaw was tight, teeth were clenched, and head muscles were tense. In fact, I had been protruding my lower jaw and clenching my teeth like a Neanderthal man. I made a surprising connection. My headache was caused by the facial and jaw tension. I was angry about the traffic pattern and inept drivers but had not realized that I was clenching my jaw. I became aware that the first muscle group in my body to get tense when I feel angry is my jaw muscles.

Now I recognize the clenched jaw is a yellow caution light. That awareness allows some options in managing anger. I can stop the escalation and relax my jaw muscles by several methods. I can massage the muscles with my hand. I can open my mouth wide and move my lower jaw from side to side. I might also think of words such as "limp" or "relaxing" while picturing my jaw muscles. I use these simple techniques while taking several deep breaths. I inhale deeply through my nose and exhale through my mouth. Thus, my focus shifts from the external cues of stressful driving conditions to intentionally relaxing a specific set of muscles. The biochemical processes in my brain are altered and my anger de-escalates.

Think about the metaphor of the river and its banks. In this physical and mental exercise of relaxing my jaw, I am using the banks of cognition and behavior to channel and manage anger appropriately. At the initial recognition of muscle tension, I purposefully change my breathing into slower, elongated breaths. I visualize a yellow signal and directly relax my jaw muscles. I continue to alter my breathing and relax my muscles. These actions allow me to maintain clear thinking to avoid irrational or aggressive actions. The exercises below will help you learn how to observe the yellow caution light and to set up a de-escalation plan. You can keep that angry river in its banks.

CHAPTER 3

Personal Reflection Activities

1. Recall the situations in which you felt angry and wrote down at the end of chapter 1.

   • Rate the intensity of the anger on the anger scale from one to ten. (Consider that a nine or ten is when you behave irrationally with rage outburst or aggression.)

   • You may record several angry instances and rate your anger on the scale.

2. Identify how often in a week you reach a five or more on the scale.

3. Can you identify where in your body you first feel tension when you become angry?

   • Write it down.

   • Think of that muscle group as a yellow caution light that serves as a warning to slow down. This signal can warn you to immediately take appropriate action to de-escalate.

4. Try relaxing the muscle group by letting go of tension in that area.

    •   Visualize relaxing, and use relaxing words.

    •   Breathe deeply. Inhale through your nose, and exhale deeply through the mouth.

CHAPTER 3

Exercises to Help Children

1. Make an anger scale, and ask your child to rate angry feelings in different situations.

2. Draw an outline of the human body. Play a game using the concept of "Where's Waldo?"

    • Ask your child to point to the area of the body that feels most tense when angry. (This is the yellow light traffic signal that tells us to stop and do something quickly to calm down.)
      You can invite your child to recall a recent angry situation and then become aware of where the muscles are most tense and located in the body.

3. Assist your child in identifying what physical sensations are experienced in anger arousal.

    • Help identify one or more of the following possibilities: rapid heart rate, upset stomach, nausea, muscle tension, sweating, shaking, rapid breathing, dizziness, or headache.

    • Help identify what sensations your child feels as the anger escalates.

4. Teach and practice intentional letting go of tension in that specific muscle group.

   • Discuss and learn what words or phrases are helpful to repeat for relaxing those muscles to shift attention from the external stress.

5. Practice breathing using a tension-reducing method of deep inhaling through the nose and deep exhaling through the mouth.

   • Demonstrate with your child, and breathe together in this manner, so your child learns how to breathe differently in angry situations.

   • A helpful sequence to strengthen this new learning in your child is as follows:

     1. Ask the child to recall an angry situation, vividly picturing, hearing, and seeing the event—feeling the anger for a minute or two.

     2. Touch the muscle group gently, or have the child touch it, and say "relax."

     3. Instruct the child to let go of muscle tension in that area.

4. After letting go of the muscle tension, teach the child to inhale through the nose and exhale through the mouth.

5. Encourage your child to practice this sequence, and reward him or her for doing it.

You Become What You Think

THE FIELD OF psychology is abundant with research and clinical applications of cognitive therapy. A major theme from cognitive psychology is that our thoughts direct and influence behavior. This basic cognitive model was originally developed by Albert Ellis in his establishment of rational emotive therapy.[1] The primary concept was identified as the ABC model. In this model:

A = a trigger or stimulus event,
B = how the event is perceived or beliefs that evaluate the event, and
C = the response or how an individual behaves in response to the stimulus.

A vitally important part in this model is the self-talk, or cognitions. If a person maintains negative or irrational self-talk, the response will be inappropriate and not adaptive. Unhealthy self-talk produces irrational behavior, but a person can change cognitions and subsequent behavior. The basic theory of cognitive restructuring techniques is that when a person repeatedly argues against irrational thoughts, the irrational thoughts become progressively weaker, and behavioral outcomes can be improved.[2]

An eighth-grade girl was brought to my office by her father for an anger problem. The girl had just been kicked off the soccer team for inappropriate displays of anger. The girl was a gifted player, one of the best on the team. She also was popular and usually exhibited good social skills. However, her action during a soccer game was so egregious that both the referee and coach expelled her.

In my office we replayed the events of the game in question. The girl recalled that a few minutes before halftime, she was kicking the ball near the opponent's goal. She was setting up her shot. An opposing player tried to block the ball, and the two became entangled. Both girls fell. The shot was thwarted. My client was irritated. During half time she brewed about the episode.

Several minutes into the second half, my client sought an opportunity for revenge. The opposing player was dribbling down the field. My client came from behind and intentionally clipped her. The opponent fell facedown and broke her nose. It was a bloody scene. The referee blew the whistle, called the foul, and ejected my client. The coach was very upset and said, "Even though you are a good player, I will not tolerate such bad behavior on my team. You're done for the year."

I asked my client to relive the experience of sitting on the bench at half time after the opponent had bumped into her. We re-created the moment and pretended she could project her thoughts onto a screen. The client complied and reported her thoughts as follows: "She did that on purpose. No one will treat me that way and get away with it. I'll show her. I will teach her a lesson she will never forget."

We discussed the degree of her anger on the anger scale immediately after the girl rushed into her. My client rated it as a three or four. However, after sitting on the bench thinking negative thoughts about the girl on the opposing team, her anger had increased to about an eight. Her negative thinking escalated to the danger point of behaving irrationally. She had *become her own negative thoughts*. It was a costly escalation. In ancient Hebrew wisdom literature, Solomon wrote, "A fool gives full vent to his anger."[3] When the girl returned to the game, she behaved foolishly.

Psychological research has provided evidence that specific types of cognitions increase anger arousal. How a person appraises the situation can either increase anger or decrease it. One type of negative cognition is *attributing a bad motive* to the other person. Anger escalates when we ruminate on phrases such as these: "He did that on purpose" "She tried to mess me up" and "You're trying to make me look bad". These phrases escalate anger. When we attribute a negative motive to the other person, we come to *believe* that somehow the person is trying to harm us. The automatic alarm goes off in our brains, preparing us for aggression. We feel justified in anger and punishing the wrongdoer.

In the previous example, the preteen soccer player attributed negative motives toward her opponent. The longer she sat on the bench mulling over her discontent, the more convinced she became that she had been mistreated. Her cognitive schema propelled her into greater anger and justified her display of aggression.

A second type of escalating thought is *catastrophic thinking*. Such thoughts result in exaggerating the discomfort and maximizing misery by emphasizing how terrible an event is. Examples of catastrophic self-statements are: "This is the worst thing that could happen" "This is absolutely terrible" "I can't stand this". What happens when someone dwells on such catastrophic phrases? The intensity of discomfort and anger heightens. The degree of anger moves higher on the anger scale. This calls for more adrenaline to cope with the immediate distress.

The mother of a ten-year-old boy amplified their problem after her son lied to her. He had been hitting baseballs near the house and accidentally hit a ball through a window. He did not think that anyone saw or heard the event. However, a neighbor had witnessed it and later told his mother. When the mother confronted her son, he denied it and blamed it on someone else. His mother became immediately exasperated and yelled, threatening to punish him. Naturally he denied his actions more vehemently. She then escalated her anger, saying, "I can't stand it when you lie. I just can't take it. You're going to grow up to be a criminal!" In her anger she meted out an unreasonable punishment and nursed her anger for days. She had catastrophized the incident, and all of her family members suffered from her irrationality.

A third type of negative thought that escalates anger is *demanding retribution*. When we say in our minds that the other person deserves punishment, we go up the scale in anger. We judge the other as a wrongdoer and give ourselves permission to inflict some pain on that person. If we look back at the example of the eighth-grade soccer player, we can recognize her escalation with the phrase "I'll teach her a lesson. No one will treat me this way and get away with it." Rehearsing such phrases made her anger rise, and she felt more justified to harm her opponent.

Our natural response to feeling injured is to demand justice or to make the other person pay. We feel justified in punishing the person, because we believe they deserve it. Somehow we perceive that our pain can be equalized or minimized by the pain of the offender. Such negative thinking gives way to revengeful acts. It seems fair that when someone injures us, the offender should also suffer. However, when we allow ourselves to think in those terms, our biochemical responses escalate anger and move us toward hostile actions.

Additionally, when we call people derogatory names or curse them, our anger also escalates. We dehumanize the other and feel temporarily empowered to mistreat them. Blasting foul language does not calm us down but tends to add to the fury. When we are bent on paybacks for the perceived injustice, we assume a judgmental position. We believe we have the right to condemn and malign. I am reminded of the words of Jesus in Matthew 7 "Do not judge, or you too will be judged."[4] Judging others only increases the likelihood that we will be judged, because hostility begets hostility. Judging the unseen motives of others increases hostility within and between us.

How we appraise a distressing situation makes a huge difference in what responses are expressed. We can view distressing situations realistically without attributing hostile motives to the other. What could the eighth-grade soccer player have said that would have helped her toward calmness? Consider the following phrases:

"It was just an accident."
"She was trying her best and got too close."
"No big deal."
"No one was hurt."
"In soccer, stuff like this happens in tough competition."
"Just calm down."

How different her behavior would have been if she had repeated such phrases during half time.

I am not suggesting that we deceive ourselves about the immediate discomfort of the distressing event by saying that everything is fine or that no problem exists. That is naïve, and it denies reality. However, exaggerating the negativity or maximizing the emotional pain is also naïve and denies reality. Appropriate self-talk keeps the focus on the present. Yes, the discomfort is real and painful, but we can handle it in a healthy way.

The intensity of our anger can also correspond to the expectations we have for any event. If our expectations are really high or unrealistic, our disappointment will be greater when the other person does not behave as we anticipated. Unrealistic expectations can be a subtle setup for anger, but realistic expectations help us cope with distressing events.

The challenge of expectations can be appreciated in the following humorous fable. A couple decided to retire at age sixty. They had a party to celebrate their mutual retirement. A genie was consulted. The genie appeared and told the wife and husband that he would grant one wish to each of them. The wife quickly replied that she desired good health and the opportunity to enjoy traveling to exotic places. The genie granted her wish. But the husband pondered the question. He recalled how beautiful his wife looked in her younger years and thought about how delightful it would be for him to travel with a younger wife. So he requested that his wife would be thirty years younger. The genie snapped his fingers and stated, "Your wish is granted. You are ninety years old."

Sometimes we get what we expect. Sometimes we get something entirely different.

Unrealistic expectations impact the intensity on the anger scale. For example, a parent may expect a child to obey immediately, without question. A child is watching television, and the parent tells the child to do a simple chore. The child mumbles something about doing it after the show. The parent demands that it be done "this minute" and becomes angry when the child hesitates or stalls. The child's action may unconsciously tap into a deeper hurt of the parent. The unrealistic expectation for the child to comply quickly produces an unnecessary and futile conflict.

A similar example is a father who helps to coach his son's baseball team. At home the father demonstrates how to properly place the glove so the child can catch a ground ball. He expects the boy to learn quickly and execute the skill efficiently. The boy tries and fails. The father becomes angry with his son, who is slow to develop the skill. In anger he scolds and accuses the boy of not trying. The child becomes exasperated because he can't meet his father's expectations. The father expects too much from his son. Both father and son feel defeated. How different the outcomes could have been if the father had realistic expectations and allowed adequate time for learning the skill.

Consider the expectation of a teenage girl who goes on a date with a young man whom she had recently met. She really likes him and fantasizes about having a wonderful time. She anticipates everything will go well and that he will meet her expectations. She dresses up, puts on perfume, and has a list of questions prepared to assist in good conversation. How disappointed she is when he arrives ten minutes late, dressed casually, and has little to say. By the end of the evening, she's angry with him. He was not what she expected. He really didn't do anything wrong, but she expected more. She feels justified in her anger toward him. The problem is not in the boy's behavior but rather in her high expectations of the date.

It is important to consider our expectations and negative self-talk. Cognitive psychologists, such as David Burns and Aaron Beck, have identified some core expectations that destroy personal happiness and hinder relationships. These expectations have been learned and form an internal belief system, a way of approaching life. Some examples of unrealistic expectations that become self-defeating are: "Everyone must like me" "I must perform very well, or I'll be a failure" "I cannot make a mistake" and "My child must be a great success". Holding to these assumptions can lead to anger escalation. Such unhealthy expectations result in broken relationships. They form impossible goals and produce a sense of failure. Likewise, maintaining negative self-talk contributes to depression and resentment. Beck and Burns have researched how cognitions impact our actions. Both of them have written excellent books that provide practical ways to silence negative thoughts.[5,6]

An example from the Old Testament scriptures highlights negative reactions from unrealistic expectations. In the book of 2 Kings 5, there is a story of a wealthy captain, Naaman, of the Syrian army. He had contracted the accursed disease of leprosy. He sought medical intervention and possible healing from the Hebrew prophet Elisha. Naaman traveled a long distance to meet the prophet and brought an array of expensive gifts with an impressive caravan. He expected a royal welcome and a prestigious reception. In stark contrast, the prophet sent his servant to meet the prince and told him to wash seven times in the Jordan River. The Syrian captain was highly insulted and fumed as he spoke these words: "I thought that he, the prophet, would surely come out to meet me and stand and call on the name of the Lord his God, wave his hand over the spot, and cure me of my leprosy. Are not the rivers of Damascus better than any waters of Israel?"[7]

Naaman was angry because in his pride he expected something different. The prophet did nothing wrong. In fact, Elisha offered realistic hope and a promise of healing, but Naaman's expectations were dashed by the humble simplicity of the Judean prophet.

Consider again the metaphor for anger—the river of anger that flows within us. What we say to ourselves either causes an escalation of that anger toward the "crazy eight" or de-escalation toward greater realistic actions. If we attribute negative motives to the other person, our anger will rise. If we call them names, we not only dehumanize the other but also escalate angry energy in ourselves. When we threaten to punish the other person or get even in some way, our anger escalates. Our internal self-talk and the unrealistic expectations we hold are key factors to managing anger.

In appendix 1 there is an exercise entitled "Negative Thoughts That Escalate Anger." It is designed to help you identify your self-talk so you can focus on recognizing escalating negative cognitions.

CHAPTER 4

Personal Reflection Activities

1. Refer back to the previous chapter in which you wrote down a personal angry situation.

   • Recall the incident.

   • Can you identify any negative self-talk?

   • Did you escalate your anger by attributing a negative motive, using catastrophic thinking, or demanding retribution?

2. Refer to the exercises in appendix 1.

   • Identify and write down your most typical negative self-statements that escalate anger.

3. What type of negative self-talk did you hear in your family of origin?

4. Identify your specific expectations when you get angry.

   • Write down what you expected from the other person.

- Is it reasonable or unrealistic?

- Modify your expectations by writing down one that is more realistic for this situation.

5. When you *think* you know why someone performed a certain action, consider that you might be mind reading or assuming something negative about the person's motive.

    - Try to identify at least two other explanations for why the person acted that particular way.

C H A P T E R   4

Exercises to Help Children

1. Invite your child to recall a recent angry situation.

   • Have the child imagine that his or her thoughts could be projected onto a TV screen.

   • Ask the child to rate his or her anger on the anger scale.

   • Together, identify negative self-talk.

2. Together with your child, use the exercise in appendix 1 to identify typical negative statements that escalate anger.

3. Assist in identifying what type of negative categories your child uses from the following list: catastrophic, attributing bad motives, name-calling, put-downs, or revenge.

4. Discuss the life experiences of the female soccer player described in this chapter.

   • Note the painful consequences that resulted from the girl's self-talk.

CHAPTER 5

Triggers of Anger

My friend shared an interesting but embarrassing moment he had in India. While visiting that country, he was invited to an Indian family dinner. My friend was eager to form new relationships, so he jumped at the chance for this cultural exchange. However, during the meal, he dipped the bread into the delicious sauces using his left hand, unknowingly insulting the host. It is considered rude to use the left hand for eating, since that hand is used for personal hygiene. His behavior triggered anger in the host and other invited guests from that culture.

What situations or actions evoke angry responses in you? It is probable that some of the irritating situations which bother you are innocuous to others. Likewise, you might not get angry about certain things that your friends or relatives find frustrating. When it comes to triggers of anger, each person is unique. Additionally there are certain cultural norms with taboos and expectations that, when violated, have the potential to trigger angry responses. Some situations seem universal in provoking anger. However, many of our most provocative situations have personal meaning and stem from previous painful experiences.

A trigger to anger can be described as some external stimulus that evokes a powerful, angry response and escalates quickly toward the crazy eight. There are certain words or actions that send us over the top. There can be a particular stimulus that triggers the adrenaline so strongly that our behavior appears reflexive. These triggers are actually learned from previous painful experiences. Our bodies remember the pain. Our minds recall the historical events. However, we may not be consciously aware of the original source of emotional pain. Thus, we can sometimes be very angry but not clearly know why.

For example, I experienced an intense anger trigger soon after my wedding, and it surprised both my wife and me. We were having a discussion and disagreed with each other. I insisted that my viewpoint was correct. My wife, attempting to emphasize her personal point, raised her hand and pointed her finger toward my face. In that moment, I escalated rapidly and loudly yelled, "Don't you ever do that to me again!"

She backed away, shocked and confused. I was filled with an anger that was very disproportionate to the situation. After I cooled down, I explained that when she pointed her finger toward me, something exploded inside. We both realized that my anger was not really about our disagreement.

I asked myself, "What was it that triggered my anger? What caused such an adverse and irrational reaction?" The answer came when I realized that the pointed finger accessed memories from my past. I recalled that when I was a child, my mother used the pointed finger as a disciplinary measure. When I misbehaved, my mother sometimes pointed her finger toward my face and said, "When your father gets home, you will be punished!" After my father arrived, Mother would inform him of my offenses. In those days a hard spanking with a sturdy paddle was an acceptable punishment. I quickly learned that Mother's finger in my face meant pain to my buttocks. My body remembered even though I had long since forgotten. But on the day when my wife waved her finger in my face, those painful feelings flashed out of my memory bank, adrenaline rushed, and my anger escalated quickly. The pointed finger is a trigger for me. It signals immediate emotional danger for me.

Triggers are those present stimuli that evoke angry escalation because they are associated with past pain, conscious or unconscious. Triggers can be verbal or nonverbal stimuli. They may be certain words or nicknames that deeply hurt. Perhaps things that you were teased about as a child continue to tap into your vulnerabilities. Triggers are almost always connected to hurts from the past. A trigger can immediately open wounds, and anger erupts like a geyser.

Several years ago I observed a family conflict between parents and a teenage daughter. The daughter was demanding more computer time for recreational purposes. She did not have her own personal computer and spent considerable time on her parents' computer. During the conflict her father emphasized that he was the head of the house and set the rules. He insisted on limiting her time. Finally the daughter looked at him with her hands on her hips, rolled her eyes, and said in a sarcastic tone, "Whatever!" The father immediately reacted angrily, yelling that she was disrespectful, and grounded her for a month. His reaction was over the top and his punishment more severe than necessary.

Upon further exploration the father recalled that when he was younger, his older sister teased him excessively. When he protested or forcefully tried to stop her, she would call for their mother, who favored her and unfairly disciplined him. When he complained his sister would mockingly say, "Whatever!" As a result that word became a trigger for buried wounds and was powerful enough to evoke a volcanic response as an adult.

Occasionally, when counseling teenagers, I request they make a list of various derogatory names and put-downs that they hear from peers at school. Then I encourage the teen to rank order them from most distressing to least bothersome. Names or phrases that are highest function as triggers for that teen. We explore the meaning and root of the buried hurts and desensitize them to that emotional pain.

Kassinove and Tafrate discuss life triggers as learned, uncomfortable events that become enduring patterns of reacting with anger. These life triggers stimulate anger arousal. Triggers do not necessarily have to be an external event. They can be a memory or even an imaginary noxious cognition. Triggers can be minor or major events but are consistently associated with emotional pain.[1]

It is valuable for you to know what your personal triggers are. The more you recognize and understand them, the greater your capacity is to reduce their power. Some persons have many triggers connected to multiple past painful events. Others are fortunate enough to have only a few triggers. In relationships we can effectively help others by choosing to eliminate certain words or actions that are painful triggers. Over time we can also desensitize our own emotional reaction to triggers. Once we have identified triggers and shared the painful experiences from which they developed, we can reduce tension. We may also use appropriate self-talk to remind ourselves that we have survived those past painful experiences. We can manage them in the present and overcome the stigma related to the past hurts.

CHAPTER 5

Personal Reflection Exercises

1. Try to identify certain words that trigger or escalate your anger.

    •   Write them down.

    •   Can you remember when you first felt hurt from these words?

2. Allow yourself to recall earlier experiences of hurt associated with each of the above triggers.

    •   Can you give yourself permission to feel hurt and perhaps cry or grieve about the memories?

    •   Choose someone you trust to verbally share these painful experiences.

3. Try to identify certain actions of others that trigger escalating anger.

    •   Write them down, and recall the related memories.

    •   Allow yourself to remember the hurts, and repeat the process as in number two above.

4. Think about and reflect on what you can presently do to reduce the strength of your triggers.

   • Can you accept the painful memory without demanding retribution?

Exercises to Help Children

1. Discuss the concept of a trigger with your child.

    • Use the metaphor that a trigger is like throwing a match on flammable material or shooting firecrackers.

2. Guide your child in making a list of derogatory names.

    • Invite your child to rank order the names from most distressing to least bothersome.

    • Ask if he or she knows why certain names cause anger.

3. Invite your child to identify any actions of parents or siblings that trigger anger.

    • Would you be willing to make a personal effort to eliminate doing that action or saying those phrases which trigger anger in your child?

    • Would it be appropriate for you to apologize to your child for these actions and thus provide a model to imitate?

4. Discuss with your child what could be done to reduce the strength of the trigger.

    • What is one thing your child can do now so it does not bother him or her so much?

CHAPTER 6

Confronting My Actions

OFTEN WE ARE quick to point out the bad behaviors of others while minimizing our own negative actions. Research on social behavior indicates that we are prone toward a self-serving bias. We have a tendency to attribute our successes to personal character traits but chalk up our failures to external factors. A.H. Baumgardner and fellow researchers concluded that we often interpret our own behavior and its causes in positive, flattering terms.[1] But we view other people's shortcomings in terms of negative traits. We believe our flaws are due to uncontrollable external events, while we take credit for positive results. In order to preserve our self-image, we avoid responsibility for negative outcomes. An interesting note, however, is that people who suffer from depression and low self-esteem tend to blame themselves for failures and perceive personal success as luck.

It is easy to focus on the faults and defects of others, especially in our families. It is difficult to honestly see our negative actions and take responsibility for them. W. H. Auden once said, "We would rather be ruined than changed."[2]

In this chapter you are encouraged to candidly identify inappropriate angry actions and the consequences of those behaviors. No matter how intense our angry feelings, we are still responsible for the actions emitted. People express anger in a range of possibilities, from total explosiveness to complete, silent shutdown. Visualize a continuum of behaviors from passive or silent on one end to aggressive or explosive on the other end. In the middle is assertive behavior. The two extremes are inappropriate and destructive.

Let us consider some passive styles of expressing anger. A person could be angry, experience sensations of the adrenaline surge, but suppress the feelings and appear calm. The individual might manifest anger by complete withdrawal into silence and refuse to interact with the other. Physiological signs of anger may exist within the person, but those sensations are suppressed. For example, a usually outspoken man got into an argument with his wife. She was falsely accusing and criticizing him. As tensions escalated, he simply stopped talking, refused to look at her, and pretended she did not exist. He persisted in the silent treatment for three days. He would talk civilly to others but refused to acknowledge his wife's presence. There was no doubt that he was angry, but he would not reveal it. According to leading marital researcher John Gottman, such behaviors would be described as stonewalling. Stonewalling is more typical of men than women. His research indicates that stonewalling significantly increases the probability of divorce.[3]

There are other passive styles of expressing anger that induce guilt or shame. For example, a teenage girl was often irritated at her parents. The conflict with her mother was particularly acute. She showed her disapproval by mumbling about how difficult life was and complained that her mother did not care. The girl also experienced tension headaches and gastrointestinal discomfort. She seldom yelled and was never aggressive. Her usual strategy was to verbalize that her mother did not love or understand her. She carried her anger inwardly and suffered from various somatic symptoms.

Another form of subtle aggression would be to instigate conflict or irritate others intentionally. Such persons may not explode in rage but rather express anger by bothering others. A preteen boy exhibited a style of instigating conflict. He was given a detention at school for committing frequent irritating actions toward peers. He persisted in doing minor things to irritate, such as tapping his foot on the chair of another student. He also teased by repeating phrases that he knew a peer would not like. He ignored the protests of others and their requests to stop. Most of the time, his demeanor was sulky with a negative mood. He appeared to gain an odd sense of pleasure from irritating others. He was disgruntled and angry, manifesting his emotions in ways that alienated him from others.

Neither passive nor aggressive styles of expressing anger promote healthy relationships. In appendix 3, "Nonconstructive Anger Styles," there is an exercise listing ten ineffective styles of expressing anger. Approximately half of these styles are on the passive side of assertiveness. You may find it valuable to honestly assess your anger styles. Assertive responses will be discussed in future chapters.

Although your actions may be habitual from repeated use, you really do have other options available. You can change something in the sequence of events and learn to respond differently in situations that cause anger.

Sometimes we are tempted to excuse our behavior with a false belief: "You made me do it" or "If you didn't act that way, I would not get angry and do what I do." Such excuses remind me of the great comedian Flip Wilson and his famous Geraldine monologue. Geraldine is tempted to buy an expensive dress. She debates with herself, but in the end she gives in to her desire. She justifies it to her husband by saying, "The devil made me do it." Too often we blame "the devil" or other circumstances for the poor behaviors we exhibit when angry. The task of honestly recording our actions in the angry situation is difficult. Nonetheless, I recommend that the specifics of the encounter should be written down. When I counsel teens and request that they do this, they usually balk or write what *others* did. They try to justify their negative behaviors. However, writing down our own negative actions can be illuminating.

What about the consequences from your actions? Did you really get what you wanted when you were angry? It is important to connect what you do with the resulting consequences. Did the method you used to stop the emotional pain accomplish what you really desired, or did the outcomes create more painful conflict?

There are two aspects to assess when we consider the consequences. The first is the behavioral results. How did our actions impact the environment? If we damaged property in the angry outburst, we pay a price for that. The consequences expose our folly. Looking at the outcomes can be a vital part of motivating us to make positive behavioral changes. It is also important to acknowledge that our anger may harm others. What relationships have been damaged by our actions? The words spoken in bitter hostility can leave a permanent scar. Emotional wounds may not be visible, but they are just as real and painful as physical ones. It is crucial that we carefully assess and admit negative impacts on others.

Several years ago a sobering story was sent through public domain on the Internet. It is worth pondering again. The anonymous piece was called "Nail in the Fence":

> There was once a little boy who had a bad temper. His father gave him a bag of nails and told him that every time he lost his temper, he must hammer a nail into the back of the fence. The first day the boy had driven thirty-seven nails into the fence. Over the next few weeks, as he learned to control his anger, the number of nails hammered daily gradually dwindled down. He discovered it was easier to hold his temper than to drive those nails into the fence. Finally, the day came when the boy didn't lose his temper at all. He told his father about it, and the father suggested that the boy now pull out one nail for each day that he was able to hold his temper. The days passed and the young boy was finally able to tell his father that all the nails were gone. The father took his son by the hand and led him to the fence. He said, "You have done well, my son, but look at the holes in the fence. The fence will never be the same. When you say things in anger, they leave a scar just like this one. You can put a knife in a man and draw out it. It won't matter how many times you say I'm sorry, the wound is still there.

A verbal wound is a just as a real as a physical one. The scars may heal, but the mark remains.

Many people benefit from recording their episodes of anger on a daily basis for an extended time. In appendix 4 there is a chart for recording, rating the intensity, and writing down behaviors and consequences. The chart also includes a space to identify negative cognitions and the deeper roots. Taking time to review each angry situation and your personal responses can provide valuable data. You can enhance your self-awareness plus keep track of your progress in reducing the frequency of anger and negative consequences.

CHAPTER 6

Personal Reflection Exercises

1. Complete the reappraisal exercise in appendix 2.

2. Consider your important relationships.

    *   Ask yourself, "How has my anger affected each family member or people in the community that I care about?"

    *   Write down the hurt your anger has caused.

3. Consider how anger affects your personal health.

    *   Are you suffering medical symptoms or pain because of your anger?

4. Complete the exercise on anger styles identified in appendix 3.

    *   Identify your most typical style and ponder how effective it is.

CHAPTER 6

Exercises to Help Children

1. Request your child to write down exactly what he or she did in a situation that caused anger.

    *   Emphasize that in each situation, many possible behaviors can be exhibited.

    *   Together identify three different alternative actions. It is not necessary to evaluate their effectiveness or moral value at this time.

2. Ask your child to assess how satisfied he or she is with the action exhibited.

    *   Encourage your child to write down what happened after he or she expressed anger in that manner. Ask, "Did you get the results you wanted? Did your actions bring good consequences?"

        These exercises can help children understand cause-and-effect factors in relationships.

3. Keep a record with your child for three weeks and review it together at least once per week. In appendix 4 there is a chart entitled "Recognition of My Anger." Assist your child daily with recording angry situations.

    Once per week review the chart and discuss together.

CHAPTER 7

Effective Use of Time-Out

THE TERM "TIME-OUT" conjures a variety of images—many are not positive. We think of the parent placing a child in a chair facing the corner and tracking the minutes until the child can get off. Perhaps a picture of an aggressive child placed in an isolated padded room describes your idea of time-out. Parents and educators have used time-out procedures for decades with varying degrees of success. Typically the responsible adult makes the intervention and is in charge of dispensing the terms. Rarely does a child make the decision.

In contrast, the model for time-out in this chapter starts and ends with the angry person, not someone else, initiating the time-out. Regulating one's own emotion is an individual task that is not monitored from the outside. The goal is for the person experiencing anger to use a time-out process for self-regulation. The time-out is self-imposed. As the person senses escalation of anger, a time-out is used to prevent reaching the crazy eight point. It is a tool to reverse the sympathetic nervous system surge of adrenaline.

Why is a self-imposed time-out necessary? As you consider the anger scale, realize that you can move up and down that scale from one to ten throughout the day, depending upon external events and internal experiences. Recall the definition of anger as a biochemical response to a perceived threat. The greater the perceived threat, whether physical or emotional, the more adrenaline is released by the sympathetic nervous system. The longer one stays in a distressing situation, the higher probability of feeling the deeper root pain and sensing a threat to one's being. This is particularly true when we feel helpless or trapped. As the anger escalates and we stay in the distressing situation, the midbrain "hijacks" the cortical frontal lobes. Aggressive reactions take over, and we are out of control. Thus, as one recognizes an increased tension, it is wise to take a time-out and leave the scene. Sometimes this is crucial for establishing reasonable self-control and protecting others from harm.

This is not a sign of weakness. Too many people make a mistake of staying in the fray to prove their point or have the last word. Such persons invite disaster. We use a time-out when we are rapidly escalating and are at a six or seven on the anger scale. Physiologically, a person at that level would be experiencing rapid heartbeat, increased muscle tension, shortness of breath, sweating, and an urge to yell or hit. When the aggressive energy is rising, move away from the conflict, take a time-out, and leave the scene.

How does a person use a self-imposed time-out? Time-out includes three basic elements:

1. Announce that you are angry and state your need for a time-out.
2. Leave the scene without blaming the other person.
3. Use tension-reducing strategies and deep breathing to calm down.

Ideally one would say something similar to: "I am really getting angry. I need to leave the scene now and calm down" or "I'm ticked off and I don't want to lose control. So I am getting out of here to chill out." In these examples the person is taking ownership for anger, admitting it out loud, and taking a responsible action to modulate. In this crucial moment, it is not necessary or helpful to give an explanation for why you feel angry. It is not a time for personal reflection. Certainly it is not a time to keep talking.

After announcing you need a time-out, leave the scene immediately. This provides protection for yourself and others in the conflict. If you can't put words to your actions, it is still better to leave and try to talk later. Blaming the other person by stating, "You make me so mad" or "I've got to get away from you" is not helpful. Likewise, saying something threatening before leaving only complicates the stressful interactions and frightens or angers the other person. Timing out is not a tool to control others, but rather a safety mechanism that prevents explosive and harmful reactions.

The third element of an effective time-out is to exercise and use calming strategies to de-escalate anger. It is necessary to do something physical. Vigorous muscular or aerobic exercise is most helpful. Fast walking, running, doing push-ups, swimming, or doing selected isometrics can be excellent. A bike ride or fast dancing is workable. The body is fired up and needs a release. The activity should be continued for at least ten minutes in order to work up a good sweat. The angry energy needs to be channeled into vigorous exercise, followed by a recovery time for our muscles.

In the past, people were encouraged to hit bags or pound pillows. Such strategies may be useful in releasing muscular tension and changing breathing patterns. However, a caution exists, depending upon what you are thinking or visualizing while hitting. Recent research suggests that hitting a punching bag while thinking of the person who provoked anger may actually increase aggression and not really decrease anger. [1] If someone is hitting or kicking inanimate objects to release tension, that person should concentrate on the physical sensations of release in the body and not focus on negative thoughts about the other person.

How long should a person use time-out? What is a realistic interval to enable the person to calm down? Certainly there is individual variability. There is no exact time that is mandatory. However, some researchers suggest that approximately twenty minutes is needed to release the aggressive tension and experience calm.[2] The length of time depends upon what you do and think during the time-out. Your body wants to act out aggressively. The survival mechanism of increased adrenaline urges you toward physical aggression. You can't just shut that off or make it disappear.

There are a variety of physical methods to reduce tension effectively. Some clients have expressed that they need to hear a sound or see something break as they release anger. For example, throwing old books on the floor or pounding a board with a hammer provides an outlet with a bang. One individual told me of an innovative and unusual method. She keeps old glass canning jars in a box in her basement. When necessary, she throws the jars into a corner and smashes them. She stated, "I have to hear the crash and see something break. It empowers me, and I feel better." As bizarre as it sounds, it actually is quite creative. No one gets hurt. It is controlled release of aggression. She feels better and is willing to clean up the mess afterward. Later she can come back and talk about the experience that made her angry.

In my younger years as a father, I kept a bunch of old cardboard boxes in the basement. Sometimes I felt an urge to kick when I got angry. So I would go to the basement and kick the boxes to smithereens. I could work up a good sweat in five minutes and make loud noises with strong kicks! Since my family knew it was Dad's way of letting go and cooling down, they were not afraid.

These strategies work effectively in the privacy of your home. But what can a person do in a public setting to prevent escalation and calm down? One primary action that can change your body's chemistry quickly is to intentionally alter your breathing. Slow your breathing down, elongate your breath, and increase the oxygen volume. Take several long, deep breaths, inhaling through the nose and exhaling through the mouth. After inhaling deeply, hold your breath for several seconds. Then exhale forcefully. As you hold your breath, the oxygen changes to carbon dioxide, which triggers a calming effect in your body. Some persons may get lightheaded or feel mildly faint while using this technique. Don't be alarmed. It is only a sensation, which rapidly disappears. The lightheaded sensations also shift your attention from the angry situation to a temporary mode of self-care.

Another effective strategy is to apply isometrics. You may be sitting in a meeting or classroom and some external event triggers anger. You feel the tension of escalating anger, but you can't leave at that moment. Doing an isometric exercise followed by deep breathing can release the tension for more calm control. An example of an isometric exercise is to start by putting your hands together with your fingers interlocking. Next, press the heel of your hands together. Push each hand into the other for eight to ten seconds. This creates a powerful isometric pressure and releases muscular tension. If you are pressing your hands hard, both of your arms will quiver slightly after the isometric action. Take two or three deep breaths. You will most likely feel a calming effect in your body and a sense of control. This technique can be repeated as often as needed. This also allows your frontal cortex to function more clearly, so you can have rational thoughts that help you make wiser choices in the moment.

A second isometric technique to use while sitting is to put your hands under your chair. Create an isometric resistance by pulling the chair up while pushing your feet downward into the floor. Do this for about ten seconds and notice the release. Follow this exercise with deep breaths.

Some people distract themselves in tense moments by creating pain. You've heard the phrase, "I bit my tongue" or "I bit my lips so I wouldn't say something nasty." Some individuals pinch themselves or dig their fingernails into their flesh. These strategies have some merit, but they also have pain. They distract and do reduce some tension, but do not produce a calming effect or sense of control. They are better than allowing the angry escalation to elevate to explosion but are limited in helping with calm control.

Another useful strategy in public social settings or at work is to excuse yourself and go to the bathroom. It makes a great time-out room. That is why they are called restrooms! Use it freely. In the bathroom you can use isometrics and deep breathing without an audience. Some people have discovered that pushing hard against the wall is a good way to release tension. When combined with deep breathing, this method reverses the escalation of anger, and your mind becomes clear.

Remember that these strategies are designed to help with emotional regulation. They prevent rapid escalation and provide an alternative to explosive actions, but they do not solve the problem or resolve conflict. They do, however, allow for time and de-escalation so your mind can think of rational solutions. After using a time-out, you can consider reasonable options to improve the conflict.

After time-out a valuable action is to tell your story to another person. Talk about the experience—how you feel and what you hope could change. Share with someone who can be an objective listener. Telling your story can release your tension and reduce emotional pain. Consider who in your family or sphere of friends is a good listener. Pour out your hurts and anger to him or her. Then invite that person to encourage you to discover a way to improve the situation. The person with whom you share should not just be an agreeable ally who parrots your position, but rather someone who can listen objectively and invite you to grow. Frequently when you tell your story, you experience more than the emotional release. You also begin to see more clearly. Your left brain and frontal cortex become more active, and you can move toward rational actions.

Likewise, praying or pouring out hurt and anger to God can be powerfully therapeutic. You can even rant and rave to God. God is not wounded by our emotions and is always present to listen and mysteriously comfort. After pouring out your emotions, be still and listen. In the silence of reflection, true wisdom and insight may emerge. Such moments can be profoundly comforting. A paraphrase of King David's lament in Psalm 32:

> Then I let it all out. I said I'll make a clean breast of my failures to God. Suddenly the pressure was gone. My guilt dissolved, my sin disappeared. These things add up. Every one of us needs to pray. When all hell breaks loose and the dam bursts, we'll be on high ground untouched. God is my island hideaway.[3]

In the calm and quiet, after the angry storm, you can think creatively to resolve the conflict.

In review, effective time-out includes the following:

a. Announce that you are angry and clearly state your need to take a time-out.
b. Leave the scene without blaming the other.
c. Use tension-reduction exercises to release adrenaline and calm down.

d. Alter breathing to elongate intake and slowly exhale.
e. After feeling calmer, quietly consider a possible solution or resolution.
f. Return to the person and set up a time for further discussion of the conflict.

CHAPTER 7

Personal Reflections

1. Are you willing to use time-outs for yourself and to allow others to employ them?

   • Would you be willing to encourage family members to think about the anger scale and use time-outs to prevent escalation?

2. Think about the words you could say to announce your need for a time-out. Take ownership for your feelings and actions.

3. What type of physical release might work best for you?

   • Try different approaches. Remember to give yourself at least fifteen minutes for cooling down.

   • Be sure to let the other person know that you will talk later, after you have calmed down.

4. Which isometric tension reducer do you like best?

   • Practice that method and remember to use deep breathing, inhaling through the nose and exhaling through the mouth.

5. Select a confidential friend or relative in order to verbalize your hurts and anger.

   • After venting your hostility and pain, listen for what you need to change and how to connect positively with the offender.

CHAPTER 7

Exercises to Help Children

1. Demonstrate to your child how to use time-out for emotional regulation.

   - Emphasize that time-out is not a punishment but a tool to help master angry feelings.

   - Help your child to select a phrase to use when telling others about his or her personal need for time-out. Some examples might be as follows: "I'm really, really getting mad," "I need a break," "I'm ticked off," "I have to go calm down," or "I'm so mad, I'd better go cool off."

2. Provide a safe place in the house for your child to use as a time-out.

   Discuss with your child that the space is a place for calming down, releasing tension, and developing mastery over anger.

3. Discuss and demonstrate several appropriate ways to reduce muscle tension.

   - Invite your child to try several options.

   - Do the muscle tension-reduction method with your child initially, to model the experience.

- Discuss that these physical releases are more safe and rewarding for everyone.

4. Practice deep breathing with your child.

- Practice together: breathing in through the nose, holding the breath three to five seconds, and then exhaling forcefully through the mouth.

CHAPTER 8

Changing Perceptions

IMAGINE THAT YOU'RE walking downtown on a crowded street. You come to an intersection and wait near the edge of the curb for the light to change. Suddenly someone bumps into you and knocks you toward the passing cars. Immediately you feel a surge of anger. You quickly turn around, ready to yell or grab the person who pushed you. As you turn you see his cane. You notice he is a blind man trying to find his way on the crowded street. Immediately your perception changes. You almost apologize for your anger as you help him across the street. You went from near rage to gently helping someone.

What did you see that changed your perception? His blindness certainly does not threaten you. What if you viewed people you have conflict with like the blind man—as struggling and needing help? Could that alter your mood and actions toward others? When you perceive some threat to your self-esteem or body, anger is triggered. Some people feel threatened in many situations. They construe the world as unsafe and expect harm from others. They seem to have a deep reservoir of anger with many stimuli that can evoke a fight-or-flight response. Other people seldom get angry. These individuals do not interpret the external events as personally threatening. They view complex conflicts as opportunities for growth rather than a need for self-protection. They may be less self-absorbed and more compassionate. They have the ability to view others in the same way they see a blind person needing help.

Perceptions can be changed. Most therapeutic interventions are attempts to alter perceptions. Perceptions are reinforced by our self-talk. We noted in chapter 4 that we act according to our thoughts. Our cognitions direct the choices. If we alter perceptions, the results will be different.

Consider the following example in which three different people experience nearly identical circumstances, but each displays a unique outcome. It is a snowy day, and all three people are shopping at the same store. The entrances and exits to the store have not been adequately shoveled and are icy. The first person comes out of the store with a package and slips, gently falling. He does not get hurt and bounces back up. His merchandise is not damaged, but he is angry. He mumbles to himself, "I can't believe they didn't clean the sidewalks. I could have really hurt myself. What jerks they are. I should sue the [expletive]. It's terrible that they are so negligent; I'm never shopping at this [expletive] store again." He stomps his feet, growls at the next passerby, and continues cursing to himself.

The second person experiences the same scenario. She slips and falls. There is no harm to her or her merchandise. She gets up, saying to herself, "I can't believe what a klutz I am. I can't even walk out of the store without making a fool of myself. It seems I can't do anything right. I hope no one saw me. It's so embarrassing." As she walks away, she feels down and depressed and avoids looking at anyone.

The third person takes a similar fall and experiences no harm. His package goods are not damaged. As he gets up, he says to himself, "Well, thank goodness I'm fine. You can expect things like this on snowy days. It's no big deal. I got what I wanted from the store. Actually, it's really quite pretty outside." He proceeds down the sidewalk with a smile on his face, whistling as he goes.

Three identical distressing circumstances—but three dramatically different responses. What makes the difference? Why is one person angry, the second depressed, and the third one happy? Yet each experienced the same distressing event. The event was sufficient to fire a fight-or-flight response, but each person's behavior was unique. This illustrates that negative events don't cause angry behavior.

Cognitive psychologists indicate that perceptions determine actions. The first man in the above example interpreted the events as potentially harmful and attributed neglect to the owners of the store. He blamed them and felt justified in maligning the perceived offenders. As he nursed negative thoughts, his anger was directed toward innocent others. The second person also felt vulnerable from falling, but she blamed herself. The negative self-perceptions moved her further toward distancing and withdrawing from others. The third individual utilized realistic, healthy self-talk. This moved him from distress to calm control. Indeed, self-talk can be a powerful vehicle for modulating the intensity of anger and subsequent behaviors.

Consider some realistic phrases that you can use to help in coping with distress. Think of phrases that could be empowering. What is something you could say that would help you feel a little more calm in that moment? What could help you feel a little more confident? In the previous example, the third individual made realistic statements: "You can expect things like this on a snowy day" "It's no big deal" "I got what I wanted from the store and the snow is beautiful". These statements prohibit catastrophic thinking that leads to helpless feelings. These self-statements keep him grounded in the present with a realistic perspective. He also offered some self-soothing: "I am fine, and it's pretty outside." These comments counter the escalation of anger. Whistling further promoted a positive sentiment. The self-statements and actions alter the adrenaline surge, calling for calm control and reasonable choices.

Thus, an important coping strategy in anger management is to intentionally speak affirmative and positive words to ourselves. In appendix 5 there is an exercise entitled "Helpful Coping Thoughts." It is a useful tool for training yourself to eliminate negative self-talk and use positive statements to improve your affect and actions.

Another approach to altering negative perceptions was developed by Steven Stosny. He discusses the identification of our core value and learning to alter resentment and hostility. He indicates that our core value is an inherent sense of deep worthiness and the ability to experience compassion. Acknowledging our core value by tapping into memories of beauty, gratitude, and compassion when we feel hurt or angry can significantly alter our negative perceptions. He encourages clients to access those inner core values, appreciate the good, and connect positively with the offender.[1] This process is learned by practicing the steps of HEALS:

H = Visualize the word "heals" in your mind.
E = Experience the deepest core hurts.
A = Access your core value.
L = Love yourself and experience compassion.
S = Solve the problem.

Old learned hostile reactions could be replaced with compassionate responses as you continue to practice the HEALS formula.

Brain researchers demonstrate that new neural pathways can be developed during our lifetime. Our brains are very adaptable, so we can learn to change old habits. Indeed, you can teach an old dog new tricks, but it takes a longer time and a lot of reinforcement. Likewise, you can alter your behaviors by frequently repeating healthy self-talk. Even when you don't feel the positive emotion in the moment, what you say to yourself over time can change your perceptions and behavior. Research indicates that doing a positive action improves your mood even when you do not feel like doing it.[2] Your positive actions can improve relationships.

Another important strategy that can alter your perceptions in a positive direction is prayer. Genuine prayer can change personal perceptions for the good. Various religious systems encourage prayer. Whether the trajectory of prayer is from an Eastern Oriental tradition or from a Western Judeo-Christian perspective, the psychological benefits are verifiable.

In 2001, several authors published the comprehensive *Handbook of Religion and Health.* They examined correlations between religious beliefs and mental and physical well-being. In 80 percent of the studies examined, they reported that sincere religious involvement consistently correlated with greater life satisfaction and happiness.[3]

A good time for prayer can be immediately following a time-out. After the initial release of tension, a quieting response occurs. The mind is clearer and able to concentrate. Prayer can be petitionary in requesting wisdom from God for ways to solve the conflict. You also could pray for the person who offended you. One researcher reported that intercessory prayer resulted in significant emotional improvements for the person who offered prayer on behalf of others.[4] Praying for the other person who triggered your anger is beneficial to reduce judgment. It encourages empathy so you can make a sincere attempt to see things from others' perspectives. Prayer may not change the other person, but it can change personal attitudes and move you toward charitable responses. Talking to God as a catharsis for expressing feelings also can be beneficial. You experience an immediate release of tension, followed by an emerging sense of peace. A person who believes in a loving, transcendent Being being can feel profoundly safe in pouring out anger through prayer. You cannot hurt God's feelings or wound his character. God is not vulnerable to our complaints or accusations. God created us with strong emotions and is certainly powerful enough to embrace them. Many of the psalms are deep prayerful expressions of anguish and anger. One of the great benefits of cathartic prayer is the beautiful peace that follows. In the quiet stillness, we may be open to listening for direction and receptive to ideas about how to solve distressing conflicts.

The magnificent prayer by Reinhold Niebuhr that is often quoted in the twelve-step programs can provide hope and peace:

God grant me the serenity to accept the things I cannot change, courage to change the things I can, and wisdom to know the difference. Living one day at a time, enjoying one moment at a time. Accepting hardships as the pathway to peace. Taking as He did, this sinful world, as it is, not as I would have it, trusting that He will make all things right, if I surrender to his will. That I may be reasonably happy in this life and supremely happy with him forever in the next. Amen.

This prayer encourages us to move toward acceptance. We are invited to let go of our demands and expectations. Too often embedded in our anger is a demand that the other person must change or that circumstances should be different. We increase our psychological pain with these perceptions. We become more anxious and try to control others or specific situations. We fail to embrace the present moment as it is. The serenity prayer can be a powerful asset to helping us alter perceptions and let go of resentment. Serenity moves us into gratitude. When we are grateful, we are not angry.

Psychological research has demonstrated that emotional, physical, and spiritual benefits result from meditation and mindfulness.[5] Developing these spiritual disciplines can significantly change perceptions into positive directions. There has been extensive popular literature written in the last decades regarding these disciplines. The discussion of their therapeutic applications is beyond the scope of this book. Whatever one's spiritual orientation is, resources are readily available. For individuals who embrace Catholic traditions, a rich heritage of Christian meditation can be explored through Thomas Merton, the spiritual exercises of St. Ignatius, the Benedictine contemplative method of prayer, Basil Pennington, Eckhart Tolle, and St. John of the Cross. Participating in spiritual direction can be life transforming. These spiritual exercises enable people to accept the reality around them and the flaws within them. They move people into a place of gratitude and peace, lowering the intensity and frequency of anger.

Historically the Protestant traditions have been hesitant to embrace meditative practices. However, the scriptures encourage meditation in passages such as Psalm 19 and Joshua 1. Jesus often went into the wilderness for solitude and modeled a contemplative lifestyle (Mark 1:35 and Luke 5:16). Recent Protestant writers who encourage the practice of meditation include Richard Foster[6] and Dallas Willard.[7]

The deepest tradition of meditation emerges from Eastern religions. The meditative practices and mindfulness of those traditions have been demonstrated to be effective in calming people, altering perceptions, and releasing resentment. Two recent authors offer practical guidelines for developing mindfulness: Stephen Hayes, with his workbook *Get Out of*

Your Mind and Into Your Life,[8] and Thich Nhat Hanh with *The Miracle of Mindfulness.*[9]

In summary, our perceptions guide personal action. We become angry when we perceive some stimuli to be threatening or distressing. Our self-talk can either strengthen negative emotions or calm us by shifting the perspective. We can alter personal perceptions and learn more healthy responses when angry. However, that requires a deliberate effort to think differently by using positive affirmations and appropriate caring actions. The practice of prayer and mindfulness are valuable in this learning process.

CHAPTER 8

Personal Reflection Activities

1. Use the exercise in appendix 5 titled "Helpful Coping Thoughts."

2. Practice saying the serenity prayer on a regular basis.

    *   Ponder the differences between acceptance and trying to control others.

3. Consider that every human is blind and in some ways groping for meaning and happiness. Probably most behaviors expressed by people in your life space are an attempt to reduce personal distress and not negatively directed to harm you.

    *   Make a concerted effort to see the good in others and name their positive actions.

    *   Ask yourself, "Can I appreciate others?"

4. Develop the discipline of meditation or mindfulness. It is worth the effort and improves your personal journey.

5. Doing simple acts of kindness toward the one who offends you can alter perceptions and improve interactions. Even though you may feel hurt and angry, you can still choose to show kindness to do something positive for the other person. Such action is a practical application of the Golden Rule and has the potential to transform the relationship.

CHAPTER 8

Exercises to Help Children

1. Use appendix 5 with your child.

   • Identify some specific, realistic, or self-soothing statements to repeat in distressing situations.

2. Discuss with your child that angry people suffer from emotional wounds that are not healed. Like a soft, thin scab that easily bleeds, some people quickly express anger because of deeper wounds.

   • Recall the roots of anger.

   • Invite your child to speculate about possible ways the angry person might have been hurt.

   • Can your child see the soft wounds beneath the surface of the other person?

3. Practice the anger management sequence with your child.

   • Recall and visualize the angry moment.

   • Instruct your child to recall the negative self-talk and feel the angry tension in his body.

- After about a minute, instruct your child to take two deep breaths, inhaling through the nose and exhaling through the mouth.

- Invite your child to replace negative thoughts with healthy coping ones.

    Suggest that your child repeat two or three coping thoughts silently or aloud while recalling the angry situation. Do this for a minute or two.

- Suggest that your child do an isometric exercise to release tension for another two minutes. (Sometimes a child may need a longer period of isometric exercise.)

- Complete the experience by deep breathing and saying "calm" while exhaling. Remember, the more skills that you practice, the greater the success. Eventually these behaviors will become nearly automatic.

4. Pray with your child about the emotional pain and for the offender.

5. Invite your child to do one kind thing for the person who hurt him or her.

CHAPTER 9

Constructive Expression of Anger

As we approach the nuts and bolts of how to effectively verbalize anger, consider the following: What are the purposes for expressing your anger? Do you typically communicate anger in order to manipulate others to get what you want? Do the actions and words you use enhance relationships or alienate others?

People can justify their angry actions by rationalizing with statements such as the following: "I just want him to know how I feel," "I just tell it like it is," or "I had to get that off my chest." While these statements have some merit, they are spoken from the perspective of the angry expresser. Such words do not demonstrate respect or value the other person. In justifying our angry actions, we tend toward self-centeredness.

Healthy anger management is not just about controlling emotions. It also involves appreciating relationships. How you communicate impacts others and either builds toward positive relationships or tears them down. Expressing anger is not primarily about making yourself feel better.

Constructive expression of anger has two purposes. First, it is an attempt to solve a problem or reduce distressing painful experiences. We want to stop the emotional pain and fix the situation. Therefore, whatever behavior we choose to express should contribute to that personal goal.

The second purpose of expressing anger is to preserve or enhance relationships. Happiness involves meaningful, rewarding relationships. The methods of expressing anger should provide opportunity for strengthening valued relationships. If you speak the truth but deliver it with negative sarcasm, you have not enhanced the relationship. The emotional impact on the other will not encourage problem solving. If you express your anger in a way that wounds or puts others on the defensive, the outcomes will be unsatisfactory. The words of the apostle Paul in Ephesians 4:29 are still relevant today:

> Do not let any unwholesome talk come out of your mouth, but only what is helpful for building others up, according to their needs, that it may benefit those who listen.[1]

We need to examine our methods of expressing anger to determine if we intimidate others or manipulate them through guilt tactics. We might get what we want in the moment, but the relationships suffer. After repeated experiences of intimidating or manipulating others, people will become weary and disconnected. It will destroy loving relationships.

A Jesuit priest named John Powell published a valuable little book in the 1970s titled *Why Am I Afraid to Tell You Who I Am?*[2] He made this statement at a communication workshop he conducted based on his writings: "The genius of good communication is to be totally honest and totally kind at the same time." That is the ideal model for communicating anger constructively. "Kind" does not mean speaking softly or being wimpy. It does not mean apologetically making your feelings and requests known. However, kindness does involve showing respect to the other and honoring the person's dignity. Again, the words of the apostle Paul in his letter to the Ephesians expresses the model of "speaking the truth in love."[3] This phrase sums up the purpose for communicating anger. We are to express our thoughts and feelings honestly and respectfully with empathy toward the other person. We voice the truth as we see it in order to solve a problem. We speak with love in order to enhance the relationship.

One good way to apply that principle is the use of an "I-message." This term was coined in the parent-effectiveness seminars developed by Thomas Gordon several decades ago. An I-message is a simple, direct statement expressing how you feel about a specific situation. It is a positive, honest comment in which you identify a distressing issue, verbalize your feeling about it, and then make a specific request.[4] In appendix 6

Dr. David R. Leaman

there is a more complete description of an I-message and how to apply it. Through using this approach, you can manifest your anger without attacking or judging the other person. This method keeps you focused on the problem of expressing your feeling and invites the other to join in solving the problem.

Initially, using the I-message may seem uncomfortable and foreign. However, with practice you can become efficient and have confidence that you are clearly communicating what matters. All skills require practice and feedback for strengthening the response. Included in appendix 7 are some practical exercises for building this skill.

Personally, I practiced specific social skills through the years by going to the woods and "talking to the trees." I would recall various situations in which I felt angry and visualized the scene. Then I verbalized an I-message and imagined possible responses. After many repetitions, I became confident and efficient. Such imaginary rehearsal builds assertiveness skills.

I-messages provide a flexible vehicle for expressing the deeper roots beneath anger such as hurt, helplessness, anxiety, and guilt. These deeper emotions are vital for problem solving and relationship building. Let us look at the example in chapter 2 in which the partner caused hurt by flirting with a younger person of the opposite sex. We can contrast two different approaches to solving this conflict. One method emphasizes anger but does not communicate the deeper root. For example, one might say with a loud voice, "You're disgusting! You talked to that woman the whole night and ignored me. I might as well have stayed home! If you do that right in front of me, then you are probably messing around with her behind my back. I can't stand you. You make me sick to my stomach! Just get out of my life."

This approach will no doubt escalate angry responses while causing deterioration of the relationship. It does nothing toward solving the problem. Neither does it reveal the deeper emotions of hurt and anxiety. The potential damage from these words may be greater than the original flirtatious behaviors. Nothing constructive is accomplished, even though some people would justify the words by saying the partner deserved it. Neither of the partners feels better, and the risk of painful alienation increases.

The second approach uses an I-message. For example one might say, "When you talked with that person for so long and seemed to enjoy it, I felt really hurt and left out. I felt unimportant to you and scared. I love you and don't want to lose our relationship. But the way you acted tonight makes me feel insecure and deeply hurt and angry. I wish you would pay attention to me in a special way when we are in public."

What a contrast! What a powerful way of being real! By sharing the deeper roots without judgment or hostility, the road to restoration is opened widely. It is an invitation to solve the conflict and heal the relationship. Using a healthy and constructive approach does not guarantee a resolution. Your positive choice and actions do not cause a specific outcome. However, it provides an excellent atmosphere to solve the problems. It opens the door for dialogue and creative solution. After an I-message, the other individual may still respond in unhealthy ways or refuse to improve the situation. You are not responsible for the choices that others make. But you are responsible for your actions and how you communicate anger.

When we communicate anger, the words should be congruent with our nonverbal messages. If we are really angry, say at a level seven on the anger scale, then our verbalizations are most believable using a strong voice. It is not necessary to scream, but raising our voice a decibel or so may be appropriate and genuine. An acronym to conceptualize healthy expression of anger is SENT. These are the components of constructive angry communication:

S = strong voice
E = eye contact
N = neutral words
T = tough posture

A SENT message is most useful when making a request for someone to stop doing an irritating behavior.

For example, a soft-spoken teenage girl was frequently being annoyed by a boy who sat behind her in several classes. The boy was not mean, but he did irritating things and teased her. Usually she wore her hair in a ponytail, and quite often he would flip her ponytail with his hand. That really bothered her. She had told him to stop, but after a while he would do it again. One time she turned around, looked him in the eye, squared her shoulders, and said with a loud voice, "I told you to stop that. It is really irritating. Knock it off, and grow up." The boy was surprised at her tough talk. He never bothered her in that way again. She had effectively demonstrated SENT. She used a strong voice in making a clear request, without any put-downs or demeaning words.

The firm voice of a parent is often sufficient to curb the mischievous behaviors of children. There's no need to yell or belittle the child. Seldom does a child need some threat of punishment because a firm request with SENT is effective.

Eye contact is important in communicating angry feelings. Most often our arguments escalate and voices get louder when we do not look at the person. Eye contact keeps us grounded and focused on the present. It is more difficult to say cruel things or yell threats when we are looking into the eyes of another human being. Through our eyes we can communicate toughness and respect while speaking the truth in love.

When using a SENT approach, your request is simple and direct without a negative attack on the other. It is even more powerful when you thank the child in advance for stopping the inappropriate action.

In some situations, an I-message or SENT may not be the most effective approach. Occasionally, children are faced with the difficulty of handling teasing and name-calling. Some children suffer deeply and feel powerless. Aggression usually does not help in solving this problem. An I-message may be limited in such situations because peers may not really care about the relationship. Peers can aggravate another person in order to get a negative reaction for amusement. At these times, an honest expression of anger may be disregarded or scorned when a child is the object of ridicule.

In situations like that, it can be helpful to empower the child, but not by overt aggression. Instead the teased child can step out of the victim role without retaliation. If a teased child manifests anger or distress, the peers could laugh or mock and do not take it seriously. Trying to use physical aggression only complicates the problem and results in punishment by peers or the establishment. However, the child can shift the balance of power by not protesting.

What can happen if the child joins the peers and agrees with them in some fashion? What if the child does not show irritation or protest in any way but rather encourages the peers to continue the name-calling or teasing? Then the child shifts the power by directing the others to do it more. Some examples of this might include a child telling adversarial peers to "Say that word faster," "Say it more often," "Say that word louder, so everyone can hear," "You are not saying that word loud enough or strong enough," "Do it better," "How many times can you say that word in a minute? I will time you. Ready, set, go!" or "You're not saying it the right way. Say the word this way...Now you try it just like I said."

These strategies put the teased child in the driver's seat. It shows strength and power. Now the child is in charge, telling the peers what to do. There are very few peers who would repeat the words faster or louder or allow themselves to be timed or counted. If a peer would do that, it becomes funny and ridiculous, so that everyone gets a laugh. At minimum these approaches change the teased child's situation from a vulnerable position to a more balanced interaction with peers. The child has the ability to change the dynamic from helplessness to equal ground or even humorous.

Sometimes adults counsel children in these distressing situations to just ignore the jeering peers. That is extremely difficult and leaves children feeling guilty and defeated when they can't tolerate the emotional discomfort. The child needs to have some mechanism in order to feel empowered—something to do that changes the repetitious pattern. Some children are gifted with humor and are able to make quick verbal comebacks, earning laughs and respect. But most children do not have the benefit of that skill. However, they can be taught the empowering tactics mentioned above with practice. The child will be skeptical initially but can benefit by role reversal and practice at home. Children can learn to say the undesirable names or teasing words and practice giving permission to their peers. With repetition and feedback, performance improves.

I want to suggest using some common sense guidelines for angry and conflict-ridden situations. During constructive angry reactions, people can communicate respectfully by taking turns as listeners and speakers. In unhealthy communications, people focus on proving a point or winning an argument, and nobody listens. Little is accomplished, and emotional distress increases.

One practical guideline when voicing your opinion is to stay focused on the present issue. Discuss the behaviors that concern you. Name the actions that triggered your anger. Identify what actions the other person took that hurt or offended you in some way. Do not attack the person's personality or name negative traits; rather, stay focused on the specific actions and your feelings about those actions. Request what you desire for future interactions.

Rarely is it helpful to bring up the past, so stay in the present. Even if the other person blames or confronts you about past mistakes, resist hurling back. Do not digress from the present concern. Referring to the past usually complicates the interaction and enflames emotions. This decreases the probability of effective problem solving. As the Proverb says, "A fool finds no pleasure in understanding but delights in airing his own opinions." [5] The technique of bringing up the past is used as a weapon to win your argument and does not promote understanding. My brother, who is a college professor, advises couples, "If each of you fights to win the fight, you both lose. Don't fight to win the fight but to win the relationship."

It is valuable in sustaining relationships to allow the other person to tell his or her story. Let the individual complain or share hurts and anger from his or her personal perspective. Try to avoid correcting or revising the story. Let the person express opinions and feelings without interruption. Try to understand the way that individual sees it. Listen carefully even though you don't agree. Remember that no two people will experience the same phenomenon in the same way. Each person perceives and interprets reality within a unique grid of past experiences. Trying to prove the other person is wrong turns the interactions into futility and escalates tension. The individual who insists that his way is right alienates others and ends up lonely. Hopefully you can develop a respectful attitude that values your own opinion and the opposing viewpoints.

There are three important guidelines to apply when expressing your angry feelings:

1. Focus on the specific behavior the other person displayed that triggered your anger. Discuss one topic at a time. Do not identify character traits or flaws.
2. Stay in the present. Do not bring up past mistakes or even use past examples. Share your feelings and perceptions in the moment.
3. Consider the other person's viewpoint. Realize that each person sees reality through one's own set of eyes. Give the other person opportunity to share his or her story and listen to his or her perspective.

As you apply these three principles, you move toward a greater probability of solving the problem and preserving the relationship. Appendix 8, "Guidelines for Expressing Anger," provides an opportunity for you to evaluate your own angry expressions.

In summary, the goals of expressing anger constructively are to solve the problem and preserve the relationship. Just releasing angry tension is not acceptable when people are involved. Using an I-message approach provides the opportunity for both parties to "speak the truth in love." Effective solutions are more likely to come from the healthy verbalization of anger. Additionally, relationships can be enhanced, especially when the deeper root emotions are shared with respect. Apply the guidelines, and your life will be less stressful and relationships more satisfying.

CHAPTER 9

Personal Reflections

1. Develop your skill in using I-messages by completing the exercises in appendix 7.

2. Complete the "Guidelines for Expressing Anger" in appendix 8.

3. After an angry situation, reflect upon your motives or purposes in expressing your anger. Clarify within yourself if your true intention was to solve a problem and preserve the relationship.

4. Practice making requests using the SENT approach. Remember to verbalize your request simply, without commenting on the other person's character. It is more effective to thank the person in advance for completing your request.

CHAPTER 9

Exercises for Helping Children

1. Explain the three parts of an I-message to your child.

   - Give examples, especially from recent personal encounters in family interactions.

   - Help your child write out an I-message for specific situations from number one above.

2. When your child has a complaint or verbalizes anger, encourage use of the I-message format.

3. Explain the parts of SENT to your child.

   - Identify that the SENT approach is to be used when the child feels frustrated and wants another person to stop a certain action.

   - Practice with your child, using personal examples from home or school.

   - Emphasize that in using SENT, no threat or revenge is acceptable.

4. Help your child identify one of the deeper roots in an angry situation. Assist child to write or verbalize an I-Message expressing that deeper root. Role play and practice together.

CHAPTER 10

Rivalry and Desire

RECENTLY I WAS observing our three grandchildren interacting together. The two boys were preschool age, and their older sister was in first grade. The boys were playing independently with little cars and Legos. Everything seemed peaceful. Then one boy looked intently at a car that was near his brother. After several serious glances, he suddenly reached over and grabbed the car. You can anticipate where this is going. Immediately his sibling yelled "That's mine!" and tried to pull it away from the clutching hands of his brother.

"No, it's not," replied his brother.

"Yes, it is. You took it from me."

His brother protested, "But it's my car, and you should not have it."

Within seconds, the boys escalated from yelling to physically fighting. Then their older sister tried to intervene. Initially she told them to stop and that they could take turns playing with it. The boys ignored her advice and continued fighting. Then she attempted to get between the boys, trying to force one child off of the other. Within a few moments, both boys turned against her. They attacked their sister, who was trying to mediate the aggression! *She* became a scapegoat for *their* hostility! She yelled and cried "This isn't fair!" as an adult descended into the fray to separate all three children.

We easily recognize this common human experience as sibling rivalry. Parents have struggled to understand and control such rivalries since the beginning of mankind. Before we consider practical aspects in managing rivalries, it may be useful to discuss the anthropological and psychological foundations of human desire.

The example of my grandchildren illustrates well what anthropologist René Girard called mimetic rivalry. People tend to desire what others have or the traits they possess. We also desire what others desire. The more one person wants something, the more powerful is the attraction. Tension mounts between two individuals or groups over desiring the same object. The tension escalates to violence, which threatens the stability of the relationships. Girard writes,

> The principle source of violence between human beings is mimetic rivalry, the rivalry resulting from imitation of a model who becomes a rival, or a rival who becomes a model.[1]

In the early stages of child development, we can witness sibling rivalry, which is based on imitating the desires of another. An object such as a toy can be sitting unnoticed for weeks in an open place. At some moment, a child sees it and begins to play; then, another child observes and suddenly becomes interested. The object has now acquired certain value, and both children want it. Each claims the right to have it and insists that it is not fair if the other child possesses it. This experience is repeated thousands of time through life. Although the objects of desire change, the imitation of desire does not.

Commercial advertisements are powerful because they tap into this basic human function. The advertisement features a particular product that appears desirable. It appeals to your desire and promises the happiness or success of the model if you use this product. But what happens when we compete for the same product? A natural conflict develops, as we believe we have the right to something valued, and others also strongly believe they should have the same desired object. Do we not become rivals and fight? We express hostility and aggression even toward our closest family members and friends when both persons want the same thing. You might recall people competing, even camping out overnight, to get the latest popular toy or electronics.

René Girard hypothesized that human civilization was founded and developed through mimetic rivalry.[2] As societal aggression escalated, it upset the stability of the social unit, and violence threatened to destroy individuals and society. However, in order to prevent destruction, the collective violence was directed toward a scapegoat instead. The violence was averted and the rivalry reduced through a common enemy. In the sibling interaction that I previously described, the older sister became the scapegoat when she tried to intervene. Both boys turned against her with aggression. She was a temporary scapegoat, which united the boys. In turn, they stopped fighting with each other. Girard develops this concept masterfully into a comprehensive theory to understand sacred violence. In his multiple writings, he argues effectively that religion serves as a deflector of violence through sacrifices. A scapegoat is identified and later sacrificed, reducing the hostile aggression between the parties, temporarily unifying them. This social phenomenon is repeated many times through the life of the community and is the mechanism of how civilizations survive.

The writer of the New Testament book of James discusses rivalry and desire in the following words:

> What causes fights and quarrels among you? Don't they come from your desires that battle within you? You want something but don't get it. You kill and covet. But you cannot have what you want. You quarrel and fight.[3]

Hostility appears to be endemic in human society. Anyone can become a rival. The desires we have are copied from another person. We desire what others desire, making them rivals. As the rivalry increases, we can become enslaved by it and try to take the desired object from the other, claiming our right to it. Jean-Michel Oughourlian suggests that when rivalry increases to the point in which a person becomes primarily interested in the rivalry and not the object anymore, psychopathology occurs.[4] He believes that we are constantly in mimetic interaction, from birth to death. It is the nature of our desire that makes us continually imitate one another, leading ultimately to hostility and violence.

Groups of individuals can readily desire what another group desires, thus unifying one group against the other. One group becomes the "in" group, and the other is viewed as the outsider or even the enemy. Each group strongly identifies with its own kind and acts with hostility toward the alien group. Groups become rivals when they compete for the same desired possessions or prestige. This will inevitably lead to violence. Violence can be reduced or briefly averted by finding a common scapegoat. But that solution is merely partial and temporary. Thus the cycle of violence is repeated.

Brain researchers have recently studied mirror neurons in the limbic and cortical regions of the brain. Mirror neurons were discovered through careful research during the 1980s. Mirror neurons are specialized brain cells involved in mimicking the actions and intentions of others through observation.[5] Experiments demonstrated that when primates observe the action of another, the same motor neurons are firing in the observer as the ones firing in the actor. This forms the basis for understanding and empathy. Solid experimental evidence suggests that our brains are capable of mirroring deep aspects in the minds of others. Research has demonstrated that reciprocal imitation occurs among toddlers regularly. Also, when humans engage in conversation, we tend to imitate the syntactical structures of language. We have an instinct to imitate one another, synchronizing our bodies and actions. We can feel the emotions of another within our own bodies due to the functions of mirror neurons.

Scientific studies have been conducted with children to assess the impact of watching violent actions in movies. Does the observation of violence increase the probability of acting out aggressively? The findings of several studies, which are highly reproducible, indicate that children who watch more media violence are more aggressive than other children.[6] Marco Iacoboni summarized many studies and concluded that laboratory research, along with correlational and longitudinal studies, all support the hypothesis that media violence induces imitative violence.[7] The American Psychological Association summarized research on violence, stating:

> There is absolutely no doubt that higher levels of viewing violence on television are correlated with increased acceptance of aggressive attitudes and increased aggressive behaviors.[8]

An interesting study conducted with third- and fourth-grade students indicated a significant decrease in aggressive behaviors by reducing the amount of time playing video games and watching television. Thomas Robinson compared the frequency of aggression in the children from a control group with children who voluntarily reduced exposure to media violence. Children in the intervention group who reduced observation of television and media for several months had statistically significant decreases in peer ratings of aggression and in observed verbal aggression on the playground.[9]

I believe that a common aim to which parents adhere is to eliminate violence in their home and community. A reasonable goal in parenting is to teach responsible problem-solving skills and encourage children to solve conflicts without coercion or force. Considering the research on mirror neurons and mankind's natural inclination toward violence, children greatly need to observe peaceful resolutions. What type of visual images do you want firing and wiring in the mirror neurons of your children?

Parents need to carefully monitor and limit the use of television, media, and video games that portray violence. Considering the impact of media and the plethora of violence manifested, parents ought to be very intentional about demonstrating empathy and forgiveness. The role of modeling nonviolence and peaceful strategies may be crucial for individual development and the survival of mankind. Children must observe compassion and imitate it in order to develop a merciful lifestyle.

Is it possible to curb mimetic rivalry and reduce violence in society? What belief system or phenomenological experiences are necessary to impact such a change? In an illuminating book on spiritual evolution, Harvard professor George Vaillant writes:

> Positive emotions—not only compassion, forgiveness, love, and hope, but also joy, faith, trust, awe, and gratitude—arise from our inborn mammalian capacity for unselfish parental love. They emanate from our feeling, limbic mammalian brain and thus are grounded in our evolutionary heritage. All human beings are hardwired for positive emotions, and these positive emotions are a common denominator of all major faiths and of all human beings.[10]

The capacity for love and forgiveness is inherent but requires modeling and reinforcement to become a lifestyle. Unfortunately, spiritual constructs of love, forgiveness, and empathy have not been explored scientifically until recent years. For many years the field of psychology and psychiatry only investigated negative emotions and diagnostic problems. The concepts of compassion and forgiveness were not considered appropriate for scientific investigation until the last two decades. Perhaps in the future, effective strategies for modeling empathy and forgiveness can be empirically tested.

These essential positive qualities are best experienced and expressed through spiritual faith. Love and forgiveness is a theme in all of the major religions. Perhaps the greatest example of forgiveness that mankind has witnessed is Jesus of Nazareth, recorded in the gospels two thousand years ago. Jesus, and later His disciples, challenged people to be imitators of Christ in words and lifestyle. A careful reading and applying of His teaching can transform individuals and society.

CHAPTER 10

Personal Reflection Exercises

1. Carefully contemplate the following questions about media violence in your home:

    • Have you considered the impact of media violence on your personal attitudes?

    • How much violence do you watch for entertainment?

    • How many aggressive video games do you play?

    • Do you think it may have a subtle negative influence on your tendency to use coercion in conflict situations?

2. Carefully contemplate the following questions about peaceful conflict resolution in your home:

    • How do you model peaceful social solutions for your children?

    • What opportunities do your children have to actually observe peaceful conflict resolution in your home?

    • Do your children observe a merciful and forgiving attitude in you?

3. Reflect upon your own family of origin.

- What sibling rivalry exists?

- What did you learn about resolving conflict when you were growing up?

Exercises to Help Children

1. Teach your children that using coercion or aggression is destructive and does not really solve conflicts.

    *   Expose them to movies and media that portray peaceful solutions.

    *   Discuss the content with them.

2. Read books or listen to CDs with your children that emphasize peaceful problem-solving and negotiating skills.

    *   Discuss the concepts and effectiveness of the strategies.

3. Significantly limit or eliminate exposure to violence on TV. Refuse to buy violent games.

CHAPTER 11

Forgiveness

WITH A CLENCHED fist, he pounded the table and yelled, "I will never forgive my brother!" There was fire in his eyes and hatred in his voice. His blood vessels looked like they were at the brink of bursting open. He told me that fifteen years ago, his brother cheated him out of thirty thousand dollars. It occurred at a vulnerable time in their lives—when their father died. His father had verbally expressed that both sons should obtain an equal share of the inheritance, but he had not clearly sealed his wishes in a legal will. His brother, with the help of a shrewd attorney, took the lion's share of the inheritance. He claimed it was rightfully his because he was the oldest. The younger brother seethed with resentment for many years. In fact, his life was defined by that incident. He became a hostile man executing revenge on innocent people, drowning alone in his bitterness.

Contrast that man's decaying existence with Corrie ten Boom's life. Corrie was a Dutch watchmaker during the Holocaust. The Gestapo arrested her for helping Jews escape Nazi genocide during World War II. She was sent to concentration camps for several years to suffer intense victimization. Her sister also was brutalized and died in a camp. After surviving the Holocaust, Corrie focused on trying to forgive her enemies through faith in God. She shared in her book, *The Hiding Place*, the difficult journey and struggle toward forgiveness. A particularly poignant moment occurred years later, when one of the cruelest German guards who had abused the prisoners approached Corrie seeking her forgiveness. Corrie believed that the love of God is deeper than any immoral behavior ever committed.[1]

Corrie ten Boom is not the only survivor of the Holocaust to emphasize the need to forgive. Viktor Frankl, the well-known psychiatrist, survived three years in concentration camps, including Auschwitz. He wrote
a marvelous and compelling book, *Man's Search for Meaning*. The book is
listed as one of the ten most influential books in America according to the
Library of Congress. Frankl emphasized that each person has choices in
the midst of suffering. He advocated that suffering could provide a cru-
cible for discovering meaning and purpose. He noted that love is the ulti-
mate and highest human goal. Love involves forgiveness, and the salvation
of man is through love.[2]

What enables a person to forgive? Does it require a spiritual faith and
encounter with the Divine? There is no universal agreement on the definition of forgiveness. Forgiveness has been expressed through religious
traditions for centuries. All major religions teach some form of forgiveness. However, the concept of forgiveness has only recently been explored
by scientific methodology and psychological investigation.

In 1986, Richard Fitzgibbons pioneered therapeutic observations of
forgiveness. He collected data demonstrating that when a person forgives,
fear and anger are reduced. Fitzgibbons laid a foundation for research on
forgiveness.[3]

The major researcher conducting scientific investigations of forgiveness has been Robert Enright at the University of Wisconsin. He identified
the key components of forgiveness as a willingness to abandon one's right
to resentment and negative judgment toward one who unjustly injured us
while fostering the undeserved qualities of compassion, generosity, and
even love toward that person.[4]

Another researcher presently investigating forgiveness is Everett
Worthington. He defines forgiveness as:

The emotional juxtaposition of positive emotions (such as empathy,
sympathy, compassion, agape love, or even romantic love) against
(1) the hot emotions of anger or fear that follow a perceived hurt
or offense or (2) the unforgiveness that follows ruminating about

the transgression, which also changes our motives from negative to neutral or even positive.[5]

Worthington further explains that with complete forgiveness, the positive emotions replace resentment and remain without negative affect toward the offender.

Modern English philosopher Joanna North developed a similar definition of forgiveness. She believes that we forgive when we overcome the resentment toward the offender, not by denying our right to the resentment, but instead by trying to offer the wrongdoer compassion, benevolence, and love. Forgiveness is a gift of compassion. We realize that the offender does not necessarily have a right to such gifts.[6]

Upon careful observation of these definitions, several common components can be identified:

- Honest acknowledgment of emotional pain is necessary.
- Forgiveness is a choice, a decision to change.
- Forgiveness involves letting go of resentment and negative judgment.
- Forgiveness fosters and seeks to replace negative attitudes with positive emotions toward the other.
- Forgiveness expresses love and empathy toward the offender.
- Forgiveness is a gift to the undeserved offender.

The process of forgiveness is more than an exercise of cognition. It involves reducing the frequency, intensity, and duration of negative, resentful thoughts. There is a cognitive shift from focusing on one's emotional pain and desire for revenge to releasing the past and embracing the present. Forgiveness is a process of honestly facing the hurts and choosing to no longer rehearse or fantasize retaliation. To forgive does not mean to excuse the actions of others, but it does require letting go of judgment and demand for retribution.

Ira Byock stated in his book, *The Four Things That Matter Most*:

"Forgiveness is a passage to a sanctuary of wholeness. It is a place of healing and transformation."[7] He suggests that through forgiving and being forgiven, we purify ourselves and prepare for more complete relationships.

In the Judeo-Christian faith, forgiveness is the central theme, especially in the gospels regarding the life and teachings of Jesus Christ. The greatest gift to be received and granted to others is forgiveness. Jesus demonstrated this multiple times throughout his life. The most powerful expression of forgiveness was in His crucifixion, when he looked upon his enemies and said, "Father, forgive them, for they know not what they do."[8]

Richard Foster writes that forgiveness is a miracle of grace, in which the offense no longer separates. It is a gift you give to the offender, releasing that person to God's goodness and inviting fellowship.[9]

Our keen sense of justice makes us cling to a belief that people should suffer or be punished for the harm done to others. We seem to be deeply entrenched in judging what is unfair and in demanding retribution. Thus, when someone offends or hurts us, our natural inclination is to retaliate.

At minimum, the Jewish Levitical law of "An eye for an eye, and tooth for a tooth" feels inherently right.[10] What's fair is fair! If you have injured me, you should feel the same level of injury. If the parental or civil authorities don't make that happen, then I have a right to be resentful and look for some way to get even.

Although we speak of love and mercy, most of us primarily operate in this legal framework. We want the offender to suffer, to pay a penalty. Thus, we can carry resentment for many years, and feel justified harboring anger. But there is a price to pay within our bodies as well as in sustaining the broken relationships. My mother used to quote the maxim "Bitterness harms the vessel in whom it is stored more than the one on whom it is poured."

Chronic, sustained anger can be a serious medical hazard. Longitudinal research conducted by J.A.Grunnbaum and associates explored the connection between hostility and coronary heart disease in children and adolescents. The results from epidemiological studies indicated a significant correlation between sustained anger and pathologic changes in the arteries of the children.[11] A similar study conducted by B.E.Ricci and associates with adults in Italy found that frequency of anger arousal resulted in increased pathogenic effects. The more aggressively people respond, the higher probability of coronary heart disease.[12] Finally, Carlos Iribarren conducted the ten-year "Coronary Artery Risk Development in Young Adults" study in which 374 men and women in the United States showed a definite relationship between hostility and coronary artery blockage as measured by the Cook-Medley hostility scale.[13]

Webster's dictionary defines resentment as a feeling of displeasure or indignation of some act, remark, or person. The act is regarded as causing injury or insult. Resentment develops over time, and the anger is stored rather than overtly expressed. Individuals who experience resentment get stuck internally protesting the angry episode. They are not likely to release their anger until they get the justice they deserve. Potter-Efron identified several common characteristics of the resentment process. He noted that resentment progresses and gradually evolves into insults. The injured person feels wounded and believes that a fundamental law of social interaction was breached. Thus, the resentful person feels morally justified in harboring anger and demanding justice. This attitude leads to viewing the offender as all bad and seeing oneself as innocent. This eventually spawns vengeful fantasies.[14]

Kassinove and Tafrate identify two aspects of an unforgiving response. One cognitive pattern is to rehearse the past aversive events in your mind. The other negative process is to hold a grudge against the offender. It is as though the perceived victim takes a picture of the offender at the moment of insult, stuffs it in his pocket, and incessantly pulls it out to seethe over the offense. The picture does not change and neither does the wounded person's image or memory. The resentful individual has great difficulty accepting the past and letting it go.[15]

Psychologists, physicians, and theologians agree that harboring resentment hinders personal happiness and alienates people. Their professional consensus is to encourage forgiveness and let go of resentment. The New Testament scriptures instruct:

> Get rid of all bitterness, rage and anger, brawling and slander, along with every form of malice. Be kind and compassionate to one another, forgiving each other, just as in Christ God forgave you.[16]

A devout Muslim in Texas recently demonstrated a remarkable example of forgiveness. Mark Stroman shot Rais Bhuiyan after the September 11, 2001, terrorist attack. Mr. Stroman committed hate crimes by killing two men he believed were Arabs and then attempted to murder Mr. Bhuiyan. Stroman was incarcerated and sentenced to death in Texas.

Mr. Bhuiyan had been nearly fatally wounded. While in the hospital, he renewed his faith and promised Allah that he would make a pilgrimage to Mecca. He concluded that his faith compelled him to forgive Mr. Stroman. Mr. Bhuiyan also made serious efforts to spare Mr. Stroman from execution. He went on a compassionate campaign of forgiveness. He told a reporter in July 2011, "If I can forgive my offender who tried to take my life, we can all work together to forgive each other and move forward and take a new narrative on the tenth anniversary of September 11."[17] Although he was not successful in altering the execution, Mr. Bhuiyan's compassionate efforts should be applauded as a compelling exhortation to eliminate hatred in our communities.

Can forgiveness be taught, since it is a volitional experience requiring perceptual changes and commitment to loving actions? Must forgiveness be grounded in trust and surrendered to God?

Vaillant argues that forgiveness is hardwired in the midbrain.[18] The capacity for nurturance and empathy exists within the human genetic substrate. He indicates that forgiveness involves two social skills that have evolved in Homo sapiens. These include the skill of empathy and the capacity to envision the future, which are keys to the survival of the human species. He further discussed that these skills have biochemical roots in the limbic system of mammals, especially primates. The capacity for a mother to express nurturance to the infant and the ability to feel the emotional pain of those in distress appear to be hardwired into the brain. However, the actual practice of forgiving others does require learning and increases from age three to ninety.

In the Anabaptist traditions of Protestant Christianity, pacifism is a major tenet. Children are taught from the cradle into adulthood to seek peaceful resolutions in conflict. A culture of peace cultivates a lifestyle in which violence is discouraged and is viewed as evil. Their emphasis on forgiveness produces a lifestyle that discourages the evil of violence.

The power of forgiveness was observed in the Amish community after the Nickel Mines atrocity. In October 2006, a man from the surrounding community shot and killed five Amish schoolgirls and seriously wounded five others. Charles C. Roberts turned the tranquility of the schoolhouse into a nightmare of horror. The violence was unprovoked and targeted at innocent children. The world reaction was universally vocal in condemning the killer and demanding justice with some form of retaliation.

In stark contrast to societal expectations, the Amish community forgave the perpetrator and reached out in love to his family. The book *Amish Grace* provided great insight into the beautiful teachings of grace within the Amish culture.[19] Forgiveness was a first response, developed from the teachings of Jesus. The Amish bishops adhered to the principle that mankind is to live by a rule of forgiving others, not by retaliation. The response of that agricultural Amish community demonstrated clearly that forgiveness is teachable and can become habitual.

In the Anabaptist communities of Mennonite, Brethren, and Quaker, violence rarely occurs. Aggressive crimes are almost nil in such communities. Likewise, the divorce rate is extremely low. These tight-knit communities emphasize controlling negative emotions and seeking peaceful solutions in interpersonal conflicts. By modeling grace and forgiveness, they raise children to be peacemakers.

Enright conducted research with children regarding their concepts of forgiveness using Kohlberg's moral dilemma inventory. Enright identified six progressive categories of forgiveness, ranging from childhood to adulthood. Children under the age of ten years old have a limited understanding of forgiveness. They perceive forgiveness similar to exacting some punitive revenge on the offender. It is similar to an eye-for-an-eye and a-tooth-for-a-tooth perspective. As they progress in age and life experience, children view forgiveness as conditional, requiring an apology from the offender as a prerequisite. When children enter early adolescence, they are more capable of understanding empathy. They can comprehend some personal benefits from forgiving others. They have listened and incorporated the values of parents, teachers, or community leaders who function as role models in expressing forgiveness. In latter adolescence, teens can grasp the concept of unconditional love and forgive others from spiritually altruistic motives.[20]

Learning to forgive is a process, over time, of receiving grace and observing merciful actions. Parents can teach children how to forgive through modeling it in family interactions.

Both Enright and Worthington describe specific steps in the process of forgiveness. The steps require a willingness to face the emotional pain of anger and the choice to let go of resentment. The sequential steps of forgiveness are similarly described by each researcher and are applicable to therapeutic situations. However, a basic presumption is that the individual desires healing within and wants to improve relationships. Forgiveness is reachable and teachable.[21]

Enright and Worthington have succinctly detailed recommended steps to forgiveness. I will briefly summarize their combined insights and recommendations in practicing forgiveness.

The first step is to recall the hurts and uncover your anger. One cannot forgive in the abstract. Forgiveness requires identifying the specific painful events and owning your resentment.

The second step is to choose forgiveness. It includes letting go of the past and deciding to live in the present with a positive focus. Deciding to forgive involves an empathic response toward the offender. Realize that the person who wronged you also has experienced pain and stands in need of mercy.

The third step is to give the offender a gift of forgiveness. This is a deliberate expression of compassion on your part, motivated by Divine mercy that has been extended to you. It echoes the Lord's Prayer: "Forgive us our trespasses, as we forgive those who trespass against us." Your gift of mercy is altruistic, without a demand that the offender admits guilt or says "I'm sorry." If possible, the act of forgiving should be a face-to-face encounter.

Finally, forgiveness involves holding onto your decision and remaining open to personal growth. In this phase, you ponder the meaning of suffering and discover the emotional freedom of forgiveness.

CHAPTER 11

Personal Reflection Exercises

1. What did you learn about forgiveness in your family of origin from observing your parents' interactions?

2. Who has been the most forgiving person in your life? How do you feel when you accept forgiveness from that person?

3. Psychological research has demonstrated that prolonged resentment correlates highly with cardiovascular and gastrointestinal illness. Consider the medical complaints you have and ponder if your resentments may contribute to personal medical problems.

4. Identify what hinders you from forgiving others. What benefits do you obtain by refusing to forgive?

5. Make a list of people who have hurt or offended you. Recall the emotional pain from these incidences. Visualize releasing the memory of that pain. For example, write the offense on a piece of paper, burn the paper, and throw the ashes to the wind. Write a letter to the offender, verbalizing your forgiveness. Later you may decide to send the letter or not.

CHAPTER 11

Exercises to Help Children

1. Try to ascertain where your child is in the development of forgiveness. What does your child comprehend about forgiveness? Help him or her to define forgiveness as a loving or kind response toward someone who wronged them.

2. Observe appropriate media together with your child in which some form of forgiveness has been demonstrated. Discuss the content as it relates to your child's life experiences. Examples in the media are *Book of Virtues* DVDs for children; *The Chronicles of Narnia*, by C. S. Lewis; *Little House on the Prairie* TV series; *The Christmas Wish* DVD; *Touched by an Angel* TV series; *Veggie Tales*; *Adventures in Odyssey* radio series; and *Les Miserables.*

3. Discuss literature with your child that has forgiveness themes. Some examples for preteens and adolescents to read include *A Priest with Dirty Clothes*, by R. C. Sproul and Liz Bonham; *Ten Tiny Breaths*, by K. A. Tucker; *The Last Song*, by Nicholas Sparks; *The Storyteller*, by Jodi Picoult; and *The Shack*, by William Paul Young.

4. Discuss historical figures and watch documentaries of persons who demonstrated forgiveness in their lifestyles. Some examples include Gandhi, Martin Luther King, Nelson Mandela, and Jesus as recorded in the gospels.

5. Practice forgiveness in your home so your children can appropriately imitate you.

CHAPTER 12

Guidelines for Conducting Anger Groups

SOME READERS MAY be interested in conducting group sessions to teach these anger management skills. Clinicians in private practice or institutional settings and guidance counselors can utilize the contents of this book in a group counseling format. This chapter includes a detailed outline for conducting eighteen group sessions. The length of each session should be approximately forty-five minutes.

Considering the research on group counseling, the most appropriate size group would be between four to eight participants. More than eight participants may be too cumbersome, and each child would not have sufficient opportunity to practice the skills during group sessions. Groups of less than four participants may be too small and limit the possibilities of learning from peers through discussion and self-disclosures. The acquisition of skills involves role-playing and practical experiences, so the feedback from peers serves as an important learning tool in the group process.

Children under the age of eight may not be appropriate participants for a group. Some of the cognitive concepts could be too intellectually challenging for young children. Also, young children lack the social development to provide meaningful feedback to peers regarding the performance of certain skills.

The gender composition of the group is relevant for teenagers. A mixed composition of boys and girls is more difficult than gender-homogeneous groups. Because of teens' sexual energy and needs to impress the opposite sex, they frequently exhibit attention-seeking behaviors that interfere with the learning process. I suggest that teenage boys and girls not participate in the same anger management group.

I recommend using the name Anger Management and Leadership Group and informing parents and teachers that this is the name of the group. Also explain to the participants and the adults that the group is designed to help children or teens achieve one or more of the following goals:

1. Improve problem-solving skills in conflict situations.
2. Develop assertive skills in relating to others.
3. Learn effective strategies in managing anger constructively.

The theoretical model for the group is a cognitive behavioral framework. The selection of participants would be based on the following criteria:

1. The child has marked difficulties with interpersonal relationships—arguing and ridiculing others.
2. The child is prone to anger outbursts and exhibits aggressive behavior at school more frequently than peers.
3. The child is more disruptive in class compared to other students.
4. The child displays oppositional and defiant behavior toward parents and faculty.

The clinician may choose to use the anger assessment in appendix 9 to obtain a pretreatment measurement. Guidance counselors could use the anger assessment included in appendix 10 to be completed by two or more teachers. These measures could function as pre- or post-treatment assessments, yielding statistical data about the efficacy of the group interventions. Some clinicians may opt to use a formal, standardized anger-assessment tool. One example of a standardized instrument for measuring anger problems in the teenage population is the ADS:Y (Anger Disorder Scale: Youth), published by MHS (Multi-Health Systems, Inc., North Tonawanda, New York). This instrument consists of a five-point Likert scale with eighty-one items and is completed by the teenager. It provides meaningful data on frequency, endurance, and intensity of anger.

It also renders scales on types of angry expression and the degree of pathological manifestations of anger. It is easy to use, and most teens that I tested were adequately comfortable in completing the items.

The group leader should use consistent reinforcement and intermittent rewards when participants demonstrate specific skills. An anger management skills record from appendix 11 would be provided for each participant. You may note that the two vertical lines in the center of the page represent the banks of the river, symbolized by power thoughts (left) and power actions (right). In between the banks is the river of anger, which flows appropriately between and within the two banks.

The best arrangement for conducting a group is having two therapeutic leaders. This co-leadership allows for flexibility in role play, modeling and teaching the skills. Also two adults can more effectively manage the behavior of the participants.

During and after each group session, individuals are awarded points based on who exhibited the selected skills. Each session is designed to introduce and enhance a specific power thought or power action. On the skills record sheet, a space is provided for recording five points when the skill has been demonstrated in the group. In subsequent sessions participants may earn additional points for using that specific skill at home or school. The leader keeps the anger management skills records and maintains an ongoing accumulation of points. Additionally, the leader should intermittently reward the participants for exhibiting the skills during subsequent group sessions or in their communities. Bonus points can be awarded intermittently to participants to encourage compliance, especially when the skills are rehearsed in group sessions. Simple rewards such as Sheetz or McDonald's coupons, candy, or small iTunes cards are effective motivators. Additionally the top two participants who accumulated the most points should be granted a big reward. This reward can be announced at the initial group sessions for incentive to learn the skills.

For Anger Management and Leadership Group

Session 1: Introduction of Group

- Theme: People who control and channel their anger are the most powerful and successful. They make the best leaders. But they have to learn certain skills to accomplish that. This group is about being in control of oneself and learning the skills of using anger effectively.
- Discuss guidelines for group interaction and participation. Each person has a right to speak and be assured of confidentiality.
- Concept to learn: What is anger? Anger is defined as the body's response to a perceived threat.
- Discuss the metaphor of anger: like a river of energy guided by the banks of power thoughts and power actions.
- Why do you have to control and channel anger? Contrast destructive anger versus constructive anger.
- Take the pretest. (ADS:Y by Multi-Health Systems, Inc.)
- Each person writes down one goal that he or she hopes to accomplish from the group.

Session 2: Rate Your Own Anger

- Review the definition of anger.

- Discuss the ten-point scale of anger.
  - Give examples of low levels and high levels.
  - Discuss the "crazy eight" point of losing control and the aggression switch, when the primitive brain takes over.
  - Group members give examples of crazy eight or out-of-control moments and discuss the consequences.
  (Note: Losing control of your anger results in losing your freedom.)
- Introduce the concept that during the day we move up and down the anger scale based on what we think (power thoughts) and do (power actions).
- Introduce the hand signal for anger control. Extend both hands in front of your chest with palms facing each other. This symbolizes the two banks of anger and angry energy flowing between them.
- Ask participants to identify situations of anger and rate them together on the ten-point scale.
- Tell participants to write down situations of anger at home or school and rate it on the ten-point scale.

Session 3: Recognize Your Own Anger

- Review anger-rating scale. Participants share anger incidences.
- Introduce a rewards-and-points system for learning the power thoughts and power actions skills. Each group member will have his or her name on a skills record sheet for keeping points earned.
- Emphasize that anger management is being in control of oneself, which is strength. The more you know yourself, the more powerful and effective you are and the more happy and successful.
- Power thought 1: "Yellow caution light." Recognize which part of your body feels the adrenaline of anger first. Discuss and illustrate. Each child who identifies his or her own yellow light earns five points.

- Demonstrate power action 1: Exhale completely and then take a deep breath. Repeat twice the moment you recognize anger rising up in your body. Five points earned for doing it in the group. Make the connection that recognizing muscle tension in the body from anger rising should immediately be released through power breaths.
- Review hand signal for the river of anger in banks of thought and action.
- Tell participants to practice the power thought and power action at home and in the community.

Session 4: Use Time-Out for Strength and Control

- Review previous session—power thought 1 and power action 1.
- Review crazy eight point and the need to prevent escalation of anger. Ask if anyone used those skills over the prior week and give points.
- Introduce power action 2: time-out. Time-out is a powerful way to stay in control of your emotions. Time-out includes three actions:
  1. Say you're angry.
  2. Exit the scene.
  3. Release tension with physical exercise.
- Introduce several isometric exercises for releasing tension, and discuss other appropriate physical releases.
- Identify several situations in which a person could use a time-out. Emphasize that a person chooses to use it before reaching the crazy eight point.
- Recommend a twenty-minute cool down for time-out before trying to talk about the problem. Each child that demonstrates the isometric exercises and saying "I'm angry" earns five points.

- Encourage group members to share any coping strategy they use to release tension.
- Practice using time-out at home or other places.

Session 5: Thoughts Make Anger Increase or Decrease

- Review time-out; award points for those who tried to use it.
- Review hand signal.
- Introduce power thought 2: eliminate negative thoughts. Provide examples and illustrations (e.g., the child who got kicked off the soccer team in chapter 4).
- Discuss three types of negative thoughts that escalate anger (see chapter 4).
- Use appendix 1 handout and discuss negative thoughts that escalate anger. (appendix 1).
- Award points for those who complete it.
- Practice time-out and "using negative thoughts" handout.

Session 6: Healthy Self-Talk

- Review anger escalation and time-out. Award points for those who used time-outs at home.
- Review negative thoughts that cause an increase in anger.
- Introduce power action 3: healthy positive self-talk.
  - ⮞ Illustrate and give examples.
  - ⮞ What can a person say that calms him or her and keeps powerful self-control?
- Use handout on "helpful coping thoughts" (appendix 5). Complete in the group.

- Discuss that violence does not solve the problem but creates more problems. Violence results in losing your freedom; thus, right thinking makes a big difference.
- Practice positive self-talk by role-playing situations that evoke anger while participants use healthy self-talk to prevent escalation.
- Encourage them to use the handout on helpful coping thoughts at home.

Session 7: Triggers that Escalate Anger Quickly

- Review and record successes of using time-outs and healthy positive self-talk.
- Review hand signal.
- Remember to give small prizes intermittently for successes or good behavior in group.
- Discuss triggers—power thought 3. Give examples and illustrations.
- Discuss why certain words or actions are triggers for the participants.
- Reward those participants who write down triggers and share with the group.
- Encourage each child to observe family members and try to identify specific triggers in them.

Session 8: Roots of Anger

- Again, review key concepts from previous sessions and discuss any efforts a child made to manage anger the past week. Award points accordingly.
- Discuss power thought 4: roots of anger.

- ⤔ Illustrate a tree with four roots.
- ⤔ Deeper emotions fuel anger, and people show anger instead of the more painful deeper emotions of hurt, helplessness, guilt, or fear of losing something important.
- Discuss and elaborate on each type of deeper root.
- Ask group members to think about which type of root is his or her most common source of anger. Award points accordingly.
- Invite participants to record incidences of anger at home or school. Then rate the intensity of anger, and identify the deeper root. Use appendix 4

Session 9: Tell Someone Your Deeper Feelings

- Review the roots of anger and what participants recorded.
- Give examples of anger, and ask group members to identify what the deeper root was.
- Introduce power action 4: Confide in someone about your anger roots. Discuss what type of person is safe and trustworthy. Is there anyone in the participants' home environment that can be trusted enough to share deeper root feelings?
- Encourage them to talk about the deeper emotions in the group so that solutions can be found.
- Invite participants to try identifying deeper roots of anger in others also.

Session 10: Change Unreasonable Expectations to Realistic Expectations

- Review any power thought or action that needs strengthened. Check progress of members.
- Introduce power thought 5: reasonable expectations.

- Discuss *unreasonable* expectations in *performance*, like learning a new skill:
  - "I have to do it well immediately."
  - "If I can't do it right, I won't do it at all."
  - "I must win. I can't stand to lose."
  - "I can't make a mistake."
- Discuss *realistic* expectation in *performance*:
  - Any new skill takes practice and time.
  - There's a learning curve. Be kind to yourself.
  - No one performs perfectly, and mistakes are opportunities to grow or learn more.
- Discuss *unreasonable* expectations in *relationships*:
  - Mind reading: Assuming you know what another person is thinking and feeling.
  - Expecting people to agree with you: "I'm right; you're wrong."
  - Expecting people to know how you feel.
- Discuss *realistic* expectations in *relationships*:
  - Ask the person what he or she thinks or feels instead of assuming that you know.
  - Realize that at least 25 percent of people will disagree with your viewpoint, and that is OK!
  - Tell the person what you feel and believe instead of making others guess about you.
- Award points for anyone who can identify a situation in which he or she had unreasonable expectations and got angry.

Session 11: Verbalize Anger Appropriately

- Review deeper roots and healthy, positive self-talk.
- Discuss any power thoughts or power actions that participants need clarified.
- Introduce power action 5: SENT messages.

S = Strong voice (but not screaming!)
E = Eye contact (but not glaring)
N = Neutral language (no swearing or name-calling)
T = Tough posture (but not threatening)

- Use SENT to communicate your anger in an attempt to stop someone's irritating or repetitive actions. Emphasize strength without threatening. For example: "I'm really getting ticked off (mad) about that. Knock it off. Just stop it."
- Discuss using SENT but also telling a parent or teacher what is happening.
- Role-play in the group. Practice the technique. Award points appropriately.

Session 12: Visualize to Improve Skills and Confidence

- Review, ask questions, and record successes.
- Introduce power thought 6: the power of visualizing.
  - ➤ Athletes visualize success before performance.
  - ➤ Visualize being in control of your anger.
- Group exercise: Take any one of the power actions and visualize successfully doing it.
  - ➤ Recall an angry situation—feel tension.
  - ➤ Close your eyes and visualize the power action—imagine doing that action very well, releasing tension.
  - ➤ Repeat the steps again.
- Participants discuss their experience and observations in visualizing. Invite each child to select one power action he would desire to increase between now and next week.
- Encourage visualizations this week to enhance confidence and power.

Session 13: Respect Goes Both Ways

- Review visualization and discuss efforts in using it. Review healthy positive self-talk.
- Discuss power thought 7: when you show respect, you usually get respect. Discuss examples. Invite the group to share ideas of how to show respect and strength without violence.
- Discuss concept of self-defense and that the use of physical aggression is never acceptable except when your body is being attacked or harmed.
- Discuss: Does respect have to be earned? Is getting respect from a man different from earning a woman's respect?
- Introduce power action 6: quiet relaxation techniques. Use progressive relaxation techniques of tensing a muscle group for seven to eight seconds, followed by twenty seconds of relaxing that muscle group. Practice muscle relaxation for approximately fifteen minutes.
- Invite participants to practice relaxation techniques at home.

Session 14: Healthy Expression of Anger

- Review relaxation techniques. Award points for those who tried progressive relaxation at home.
- Introduce power action 7: I-messages.
- See handout in appendix 6. Define and illustrate the three parts of an I-message.
- Discuss that in this approach, you share the root feeling and make an honest request for the purpose of solving a problem and preserving a relationship.
- Group practice with I-message. Leader verbalizes a situation, and participants write an I-message. Have some members read their responses; leader discusses.

- Visualize successfully using an I-message.
- Hand out a practice exercise sheet for using I-messages (appendix 7). Change the examples to fit the youths' life experiences.

Session 15: Continue Healthy Expression of Anger

- Review the definition of the I-message and discuss attempts to use it at home.
- Practice using I-messages in the group.
- Visualize and practice in dyads or triads. Award points accordingly.
- Encourage participants to use I-messages at home and at school.

Session 16: Healing Broken Relationships

- Review any power thought or power action that participants need to strengthen.
- Introduce power thought 8—letting go of resentment—and discuss refusal to seek revenge.
- Visualize resentment as some ugly or undesirable thing in your body, and then visualize releasing it; watch it leave your body, or visualize holding the resentment in your tightly closed fist and then letting it go by opening the hand.
- Discuss the guidelines for expressing anger in appendix 8. Ask participants to rate themselves on the five items.

Session 17: Apologize for Mistreating Someone

- Review the guidelines for expressing anger.
- Practice using the guidelines by role-playing incidences of anger.

- Introduce power action 8: apologizing.
- Discuss what the differences are between a phony apology and a genuine apology.
- Discuss how saying "I'm sorry" could be manipulative and self-serving.
- Demonstrate a simple, genuine apology that does not put blame on another person.
- A healthy apology requires inner strength and is an important first step to making amends in a relationship.
- Invite participants to write down the names of people they have offended. Ask if they would be willing to apologize and do something kind for that person.

Session 18: Forgive and Make Amends

- Review participants' experiences from the week regarding apologies and expressing anger constructively.
- Introduce the concept of forgiveness and obtain definitions of it from group members.
- Inquire if any of the group participants have experienced being forgiven and how that feels.
- Is forgiving someone a strength or weakness?
- Discuss an example of forgiveness that was demonstrated in a movie, a television show, or a book.
- Discuss the steps to forgiveness written at the end of chapter 11 in this book.
- Invite participants to explore their personal needs to forgive by having further conversations with someone they can trust.

APPENDIX 1

Negative Thoughts that Escalate Anger

1. "You make me feel so bad!" or "You make me so mad!"

2. "You did this on purpose just to provoke or hurt me!"

3. "It's not fair. You are not going to get away with this!"

4. "You are wrong, and I'll prove it!"

5. "You should be punished or taught a lesson!"

6. "This is bullcrap. The only thing you care about is yourself!"

7. "You stupid jerk. You are such a _____!"

8. "You always _____."

    or, "You never _____."

9. "No one is going to treat me that way!"

10. "There you go again! You're not gonna do this to me again!"

11. Add your own negative self-statements:

    a. _____
    b. _____
    c. _____

APPENDIX 2

Reappraising Angry Episodes

1. Write down a recent situation in which you became angry. What *behaviors* did the other person do that evoked your anger?

2. How did you *appraise* the event? What words did you think or say to describe it? What did you *believe* about the person?

3. How did your response contribute to the angry episode? Did your response have an escalating or a calming influence?

4. Consider some *alternative and realistic* ways of responding. If you were paid money to endure the distressing episode, how much could you tolerate it?

5. Write down two positive aspects about the other person and the event. Think about that.

APPENDIX 3

Nonconstructive Anger Styles

The following are some ineffective or destructive styles of expressing anger. Read each one and honestly consider the extent that you use that style when dealing with your angry feelings. Select and rank order (1, 2, 3, etc.) the three styles that are most typical for you.

_____ 1. <u>Silent Withdrawal</u>: Avoid arguing, keep anger inside, and act as though nothing bothers you. Refuse to talk. Sulk and hide.

_____ 2. <u>Excedrin Approach</u>: Body complaints, especially headaches related to suppressing anger. "I feel sick. He gives me a pain."

_____ 3. <u>Explosive Temper</u>: Erupt with rage. Yell and curse, sometimes with a physical aggression toward objects or people. Create a scene and dramatize the anger.

_____ 4. <u>Attacking Blame</u>: Place blame on the other person. "It's your fault that I'm mad." Act like the other person made you do it.

_____ 5. <u>Seeking Revenge</u>: Plot how to get even. Directly or indirectly try to hurt or punish the other.

_____ 6. <u>Nagging Talker</u>: Frequently nag about things. Whine and complain. Harp about the mistakes or weaknesses of others.

_____ 7. <u>Sarcastic Humor</u>: Sting others by making jokes about inadequacies or qualities in others, and put others on defensive. Use subtle put-downs through sarcasm.

_____ 8. <u>Passive Aggressive</u>: Deny anger. Pretend to be considerate, but reveal anger indirectly through acts such as forgetting, being tardy, losing things, and withholding sex. These behaviors are habitual.

_____ 9. <u>Irritating Instigator</u>: Look for fights. Pick at people with intent of stirring up anger. Seek opportunities to irritate others or to have an excuse "to get mad."

_____ 10. <u>Placating Stuffer</u>: Shove angry feelings down inside. Try to please others by being nice and complying. Don't allow oneself to feel angry. Avoid conflict as much as possible.

APPENDIX 4

Recognition of My Anger

Situation (*Possible triggers*)	Rating (*1–10*)	Behavior	Outcomes	Negative Cognition (*Self-talk*)	Emotional Pain (*Root*)

Helpful Coping Thoughts

1. Just as long as I keep my cool, I'm in control.
2. I can't change another person with anger. I *can* change my response.
3. I can find a way to say what I want without being loud or mean.
4. Stay calm, make no judgments, and do not blame.
5. I'll stay rational—my anger does not solve anything.
6. It's just not worth getting so angry.
7. I can handle this. I am responsible for my behavior.
8. I can't expect people to act the way I want them to.
9. I don't have to take this so seriously.
10. I have a plan to handle this.
11. Others: _____

Action:

Write down the three general coping thoughts that most appeal to you:

1. _____

2. _____

3. _____

Memorize the three coping thoughts you've selected.

I-Messages by Definition

An I-message is simply a statement from me to you that lets you know just *how I feel*. It may also tell you *why* I feel that way. The statement generally starts simply with "I" and is followed by a clear, straightforward *feeling* message. For example: "When I want to talk, and you walk away, I feel hurt and rejected."

Components of an I-message are as follows:

1. Factual nonblaming description of specific behavior:

    "When you are late for dinner…"

2. An honest, nonblaming sharing of resulting feelings:

    "…I am scared you might have had an accident, and I am also hurt that you didn't call me."

3. A straightforward, honest description of real demands:

    "What I want you to do is to call me when you know you'll be late."

I-messages:

- are positive communication and nourish honest feelings;
- help to bring solutions through communication, versus "you-messages" that are destructive, explosive, and can lead to anger and fighting;
- do not personally attack or criticize like a you-message does;
- are clear, concise and honest—an accurate awareness of your present feelings; and
- are essential to sharing intimately.

Below is an example of how an I-message is less accusatory than some of the usual ways we tend to communicate. Notice how clear and straightforward the message is when sent as an I-message.

You-message
"You're always slamming the door and waking the baby. You have no consideration for others."

<u>I-message</u>
"I am very tired and need some time to myself while the baby is sleeping. I would like you to close the door quietly so that she doesn't wake up."

APPENDIX 7

Practice Exercises for Using the I-Message

An effective I-message has three basic components:

1. A brief description of the distressing event
2. A verbalization of your feelings
3. A simple request

Example: While you are talking, a person repeatedly interrupts you, cutting off your thoughts and challenging your viewpoints. In several minutes of conversation, you have not been able to complete one idea because of the interruptions. How would you feel? What would you request?

A reasonable response would be,

"When you frequently interrupt me:..."

- I feel angry and disrespected.
- I wish you would just wait until I'm done talking before you speak."

Practice: In the following distressing situations, develop your skills by writing an I-message that has all three components. Try to identify the deep-root emotion and express it.

1. Your daughter often comes into your room and uses cosmetics or clothes without asking and does not return them.

   Identify your feelings: _____

   Write an I-message: _____

2. Your partner clutters the house and does not put things away. Your partner also misplaces important information because of lack of organization. You have tried to improve your mate with minimal success.

   Identify your feelings: _____

   Write an I-message: _____

3. You have confided something very private to a good friend. A couple of weeks later, a casual acquaintance says something to you about that private information. You did not want others to know about it, especially this particular person.

   Identify your feelings: _____

   Write an I-message: _____

4. When you meet with the head of the organization, you discover that a promotion was given to someone less qualified, and you are asked to be the assistant.

   Identify your feelings: _____

   Write an I-message: _____

5. At work some people go overboard in teasing and doing annoying things. Your frustration has been mounting. The final straw occurs when one of them takes something important from your workspace and hides it for a joke. You need the item to proceed with your work responsibilities that day.

    Identify your feelings: _____

    Write an I-message: _____

Please note: As you write the I-messages, try to visualize saying those words in each situation. Imagine how you would like to communicate them. Visualize doing it confidently and successfully. Rehearsing in this way strengthens your skills.

APPENDIX 8

Guidelines for Expressing Anger

Using the scale below, rate yourself on how often you've used each of these five guidelines during the past three months:

never   *rarely*   *occasionally*   *frequently*   *always*

1. Clearly define what is your discomfort. State what specific actions are distressful.

2. Focus on the behaviors, and do not name personality flaws or attack the defects of the other person.

3. Stay focused on the present concern. Do not bring up past issues or experiences.

4. Listen respectfully to the other person's viewpoint and perceptions.

5. Use the I-message format to express your feelings and requests.

Anger Assessment

Name of Child: _____   **Name of Parent:** _____

Child's Date of Birth: _____

Home Phone Number: _____   **Date:** _____

Medications (Name and Dosage): _____

_____

Please rate your child according to the behaviors and attitudes you have observed at home or in public. Place the appropriate number in the blank space at the right.

Never				**Almost Always (Daily)**
1	2	3	4	5

1. Teases and name calls _____

2. Blames others in disagreements _____

3. Physically fights (punches, kicks, shoves family members) _____

4. When teased, threatens to use physical retaliation _____

5. Overreacts angrily to accidents   _____

6. Gets into verbal arguments with parents or siblings   _____

7. Breaks rules in games   _____

8. Curses at parents   _____

9. Uses physical force to dominate siblings   _____

10. Starts fights with peers   _____

11. Refuses to comply   _____

12. When angry, breaks, throws, or destroys objects   _____

13. When frustrated, yells or swears   _____

14. Responds angrily when fails at something   _____

15. Incites others to gang up on a sibling or peer   _____

Anger Assessment for Student by Teacher

Student Name: _____   **Date:** _____

Faculty Name: _____

Please rate this student according to the behaviors and attitudes you have observed in the classroom or on school property. Place the appropriate number in the blank space at the right.

Never				**Almost Always (Daily)**
1	2	3	4	5

1. Teases and name calls   _____

2. Blames others in disagreements   _____

3. Physically fights (punches, kicks, shoves, etc.)   _____

4. When teased, threatens to use physical retaliation   _____

5. Overreacts angrily to accidents   _____

6. Gets into verbal arguments   _____

7. Breaks rules in games   _____

8. Curses at faculty   _____

9. Uses physical force to dominate   _____

10. Starts fights with peers   _____

11. Refuses to comply   _____

12. Threatens and bullies others   _____

13. When frustrated, yells and swears   _____

14. Responds angrily when fails at something   _____

15. Incites others to gang up on a peer   _____

Anger Management Skills Record

"I AM IN CONTROL"

Power Thoughts	Power Actions

Power Thoughts

____ 1. Recognize body temperature and use "yellow light"

____ 2. Eliminate negative thoughts

____ 3. Identify triggers

____ 4. Identify root of anger

____ 5. Use reasonable expectations

____ 6. Visualize success

____ 7. Respect each person

____ 8. Let go of resentment

Power Actions

____ 1. Exhale, and then take deep breaths

____ 2. Use time-out and power release

____ 3. Express healthy, positive self-talk

____ 4. Tell someone your root feeling

____ 5. S.E.N.T

____ 6. Use a relaxation technique

____ 7. Verbalize I-messages

____ 8. Apologize for mistreating someone

Forgive...and...be free!

Student Name _____

References

Chapter 1

1. Howard Kassinove and Raymond Tafrate, *Anger Management* (Atascadero, CA: Impact Publishers, 2002), 7.

2. Ronald T. Potter-Efron, *Handbook of Anger Management* (New York: Haworth Clinical Press, 2005), 2.

3. Jim Larson and John Lockman, *Helping Schoolchildren Cope With Anger: A Cognitive-Behavioral Intervention* (New York: Guilford Press, 2002).

4. Ephesians 4:26 (New International Version).

Chapter 2

1. Sandra P. Thomas, *Women and Anger* (New York: Springer Publishing Company, 1993).

2. Steven Stosny, *You Don't Have to Take It Anymore* (New York: Free Press, 2006).

Chapter 3

1. Stosny, *You Don't Have to Take It Anymore.*

Chapter 4

1. Albert Ellis, *Humanistic Psychotherapy: The Rational Emotive Approach* (New York: Julian Press, 1973).

2. Rian McMullin, *Cognitive Therapy Techniques* (New York: W. W. Norton, 1986).

3. Proverbs 29:11 (New International Version).

4. Matthew 7:1 (New International Version).

5. David D. Burns, *Ten Days to Self-Esteem* (Fort Mill, SC: Quill, 1999).

6. David D. Burns and Aaron T. Beck, *Feeling Good: The New Mood Therapy* (New York: William Morrow and Company, 1980).

7. 2 Kings 5:11 (New International Version).

Chapter 5

1. Kassinove and Tafrate, *Anger Management.*

Chapter 6

1. A. H. Baumgardner, P. P. Hepper, and R. M. Arkin, "Role of Causal Attribution in Personal Problem Solving," *Journal of Personality and Social Psychology* 50 (1986): 636–643.

2. W. H. Auden, *The Age of Anxiety: A Baroque Eclogue* (Princeton University Press, 2011).

3. John Gottman, *The Marriage Clinic* (New York: W. W. Norton & Company, 1999).

Chapter 7

1. B. J. Bushman, R. F. Baumeister, and A. D. Stuck, "Catharsis, Aggression, and Persuasive Influence: Self-Fulfilling or Self-Defeating Prophecies?" *Journal of Personality and Social Psychology* 76 (1999): 367–376.

2. Gottman, *The Marriage Clinic*.

3. Psalm 32:5–7 (The Message).

Chapter 8

1. Stosny, *You Don't Have to Take It Anymore*.

2. John Arden, *Rewire Your Brain* (New York: Wiley and Sons, 2010).

3. Harold G. Koenig, Michael E. McCullough, and David B. Larson, *Handbook of Religion and Health* (Oxford University Press, 2001).

4. S. O'Laoire, "An Experimental Study of the Effects of Distant, Intercessory Prayer on Self-Esteem, Anxiety, and Depression," *Alternative Therapies in Health and Medicine* 3 (1997): 38–53.

5. Steven Hayes, Follette, V. M. and Lineham, M., eds. *Mindfulness and Acceptance: Expanding the Cognitive Behavioral Tradition* (New York: Guilford Press, 2004).

6. Richard Foster, *Prayer: Finding the Heart's True Home* (San Francisco: HarperCollins, 1992).

7. Dallas Willard, *The Spirit of the Disciplines* (San Francisco: Harper and Row, 1998).

8. Stephen C. Hayes, *Get Out of Your Mind and Into Your Life* (Oakland, CA: New Harbinger, 2005).

9. Thich Nhat Hanh, *The Miracle of Mindfulness* (Boston: Beacon Press, 1976).

Chapter 9

1. Ephesians 4:29 (New International Version).

2. John Powell, *Why Am I Afraid To Tell You Who I Am?* (Allen, TX: Tabor Publishing, 1969).

3. Ephesians 4:15 (New International Version).

4. Thomas Gordon, *Parent Effectiveness Training* (New York: Random House, 1970).

5. Proverbs 18:2 (New International Version).

Chapter 10

1. Rene Girard, *I See Satan Fall Like Lightening* (Maryknoll, NY: Orbis Books, 2002), 11.

2. Rene Girard, *Violence and the Sacred* (Baltimore, MD: Johns Hopkins University Press, 1997).

3. James 4:1–2 (New International Version).

4. Jean-Michel Oughourlian, *The Genesis of Desire* (East Lansing: Michigan State University Press, 2010).

5. Marco Iacoboni, *Mirroring People* (New York: Picador, 2008).

6. J. Milavskyy, J. andR. Kessler, R. and H. Stripp, H. (1982). *Television and Aggression: A Panel Study* (New York: Academic Press, 1982).

7. Iacoboni, *Mirroring People*.

8. American Psychological Association, "Violence and Youth: Psychology's Response," *Summary of Report on the APA Commission on Violence and Youth*, Vol. 1 (1993): 33.

9. Thomas Robinson, "Intervention to Reduce Media Viewing Improves Aggressive Children's Behavior," *Archives of Pediatric and Adolescent Medicine* 155 (2001): 17–23.

10. George E. Vaillant, *Spiritual Evolution: How We Are Wired for Faith, Hope, and Love* (United Kingdom: Harmony Publishing Company, 2000), 3.

Chapter 11

1. Corrie ten Boom, *The Hiding Place* (Grand Rapids, MI: Chosen Books, 1971).

2. Viktor Frankl, *Man's Search For Meaning: An Introduction to Logotherapy* (New York: Washington Square Press, 1969).

3. Richard P. Fitzgibbons, "The Cognitive and Emotional Uses of Forgiveness in the Treatment of Anger," *Psychotherapy* 23 (1986): 629–633.

4. Robert Enright, *Forgiveness is a Choice* (Washington, DC: American Psychological Association, 2001).

5. Everett Worthington, *Forgiving and Reconciling* (Downers Grove, IL: Intervarsity Press, 2003), 41.

6. Joanna North, "Wrongdoing and Forgiveness," *Philosophy* 62, no. 242 (1987): 499–508.

7. Ira Byock, *The Four Things That Matter Most* (New York: Free Press, 2004), 40.

8. Luke 23:24 (New International Version).

9. Richard Foster, *Prayer: Finding the Heart's True Home* (San Francisco: HarperCollins, 1992).

10. Leviticus 24:19–20 (New International Version).

11. J. A. Grunbaum, Vernon, S. W. and C. M. Clasen, C. M. (1997). "The Association Between Anger and Hostility and Risk Factors for Coronary Heart Disease in Children and Adolescents: A Review," *Annals of Behavioral Medicine* 19 (1997): 179–189.

12. B. Ricci, E. Pio, P. Gremigni, G. Bertolotti, and A. M. Zotti, "Dimensions of Anger and Hostility in Cardiac Patients," *Psychotherapy and Psychosomatics* 64 (1995): 162–172.

13. Carlos Iribarren, "Coronary Artery Risk Development in Young Adults (CARDIA)," *Journal of American Medical Association* 283 (2000): 2546–2551.

14. Potter-Efron, *Handbook of Anger Management.*

15. Kassinove and Tafrate, *Anger Management.*

16. Ephesians 4:31–32 (New International Version).

17. Alastair Leithead, "Texas death row killer forgiven by shooting victim," *BBC News* (July 19, 2011), www.bbc.com/news/world-us-canada-14199078.

18. Vaillant, *Spiritual Evolution.*

19. Donald Kraybill, Steven Nolt, and David Weaver-Zercher, *Amish Grace: How Forgiveness Transcended Tragedy* (New York: John Wiley and Sons, 2007).

20. Enright, *Forgiveness is a Choice.*

21. Worthington, *Forgiving and Reconciling.*

Made in the USA
Charleston, SC
29 November 2015